POVERTY IN AN AFFLUENT SOCIETY

INQUIRY INTO CRUCIAL AMERICAN PROBLEMS
Series Editor *JACK R. FRAENKEL*

POVERTY IN AN AFFLUENT SOCIETY:

Personal Problem or National Disgrace?

Second Edition

David A. Durfee

Social Studies Chairman
Sleepy Hollow High School
The Tarrytowns, N.Y.

PRENTICE-HALL, INC., ENGLEWOOD CLIFFS, N.J.

Photo Credits

De Wys, Inc., viii; The Bettman Archive, Inc., 6; Culver Pictures, Inc., 10; Jason Laure from Woodfin Camp & Associates, 19; Wide World Photos, 21, 30, 37, 62, 85, 88, 89, 93; Ted Ward from De Wys, Inc., 26; Paul Conklin from Monkmeyer Press, Photo Service, 39, 102; Van Bucher from Rapho/Photo Researchers, Inc., 43, 74; © 1975 Judy Gurovitz from Rapho/Photo Researchers, Inc., 50; H. Kubota from Magnum Photos, Inc., 56; Bruce Roberts from Rapho/Photo Researchers, Inc., 72; Hugh Rogers from Monkmeyer Press Photo Service, 109; Leo De Wys, Inc., 110.

Library of Congress Cataloging in Publication Data
DURFEE, DAVID A
    Poverty in an affluent society.
    (Inquiry into crucial American problems)
    Bibliography: p.
1. Poor—United States. I. Title.
HC110.P6D87 1977   301.44'1   76-8929
ISBN 0-13-693663-6
ISBN 0-13-693655-5 pbk.

Prentice-Hall International, Inc.,
London
Prentice-Hall of Australia, Pty. Ltd.,
Sydney
Prentice-Hall of Canada, Ltd.,
Toronto
Prentice-Hall of India Private Ltd.,
New Delhi
Prentice-Hall of Japan, Inc.,
Tokyo

PREFACE

1931036

The series INQUIRY INTO CRUCIAL AMERICAN PROBLEMS focuses upon a number of important contemporary social and political issues. Each book presents an in-depth study of a particular problem, selected because of its pressing intrusion into the minds and consciences of most Americans today.

A number of divergent viewpoints, from a wide variety of different *kinds* of sources, encourage discussion and reflection, and help students to realize that the same problem may be viewed from a number of different vantage points. Of major concern throughout is a desire to help students realize that honest individuals may differ in their views.

After a short introductory chapter, Chapter Two presents a brief historical and contemporary background on the central issue. The chapters that follow explore the issue in detail. A conscientious effort has been made to avoid endorsing any one viewpoint as the "right" viewpoint, or to judge the arguments of particular individuals or organizations. Conclusions are not drawn for students. Instead, a variety of positions are presented, along with open-ended questions and involving activities, so that students can arrive at and evaluate their own conclusions.

Great care has been taken to make these books substantive, highly interesting to students, and readable. Whenever possible, dialogues involving or descriptions showing actual people responding and reacting to problematic situations are presented. Briefly, each book

- presents divergent, conflicting views on the issue under consideration;

- gives as many perspectives and dimensions on the issue as space permits;

- presents articles on a variety of reading levels;

- deals with real people involved in situations of concern to them;

- includes questions which encourage thought about and discussion of the various viewpoints expressed;

- includes activities that involve students and lead to further consideration of the problems presented;

- provides cartoons, photographs, and other illustrations to help students arrive at a more complete understanding of the issue under study.

JACK R. FRAENKEL
Series Editor

CONTENTS

1
INTRODUCTION

In the spring of 1974 Americans were startled by the news that Patricia Hearst, daughter of millionaire newspaper publisher Randolph Hearst of California, had been kidnapped by a group calling itself the Symbionese Liberation Army, or SLA. The primary ransom demand of the group was the distribution of $70 worth of groceries to each poor person or member of a minority group in the state. In an effort to justify its actions, the SLA stated that all peaceful means of achieving justice for the poor had been tried and had failed because the comfortable people of America just didn't care.

Although the methods used by the SLA were generally condemned, the action did bring new attention to the problem of poverty in a rich America. Important questions were raised: Were there really so many poor in America that feeding just those in the one state of California could cost an estimated hundreds of millions of dollars? Was poverty a serious enough problem to cause people even to think of such dreadful measures?

Just about everyone, of course, had known about the extent and seriousness of poverty in the depression years of the 1930s. Then the nation's attention had shifted to World War II. After that war poverty was generally thought of as something that happened to Asians or to people living in areas ravaged by war, not something that happened here.

Poverty in America was rediscovered in 1960. In that year John F. Kennedy went into West Virginia looking for votes that could make him the Democratic nominee for President. He found the votes he was looking for. He also found poverty.

There were not just a few poor people living in the hills and mountains of West Virginia in 1960, there were thousands. John Kennedy (and many others) also found poor people in New York. They found people living in want in Mississippi. They looked in California and North Dakota and in all of the rest of the 50 states of the Union. In every state they found poverty.

The evidence that poverty was widespread increased. One victim of poverty in a Chicago slum area reported:

[1]Excerpted from Kenan Heise, *They Speak for Themselves* (Chicago, Ill.: The Young Christian Workers, 1965).

I would say that there must be 100 people in this neighborhood who go to one garbage can or the other for food regularly. I would say 100 at least. A lot of them are really dependent on that food. When they come to the end of their welfare check, and if they dig diligently, they can live it out.[1]

Another victim, a migrant farm worker, described conditions in a camp:

The hollow square where the truck stood was paved with dusty rubble. Three long wooden shacks, once, but not recently, whitewashed, bounded three sides of the square; the fourth side lay open to a beanfield. A patch of woods concealed the camp from the highway.

Each shack had a row of doors opening into a square. A scrawly number painted in black identified each door. All the threes were painted backward, and on each six and each nine the circle appeared on the wrong side of the stem as though children had been practicing writing in a looking glass. The doorsills were a good foot from the ground and there were no steps. To serve instead, some had cement blocks laid in front of them; a few had makeshift ramps of boards; three or four had inverted washtubs; some had nothing at all. Beside every door there was a window. There were no screens. Here and there stood trash cans spilling over with rubbish waiting to be hauled away. None of the cans had lids, and it all looked and smelled like the accumulation of several days. . . .

The morning sun poured hotly down on a sprawling woodpile; on a clothesline hung with diapers and little girls' dresses; on a derelict washing machine; on four slender iron pipes, one in each corner of the square, each rising two feet high and each topped by a water faucet. In the middle of the square a rusty, old-fashioned iron cookstove rested on the ground against the wall of a shanty. The shanty had a stovepipe in the roof, advertising that there was at least one more stove inside. That wasn't all that was in there, either, because through the shanty's open door a voice out of a jukebox told the world, *I've got everything, I've got you.*[2]

Another resident of Chicago described the effect of being poor in a rich society, saying, "I'm nothing more than a dishwasher. I make $8 a night, six nights a week. My take home pay is around $42. I'm nothing. I'm like an ant. They can step on me anytime they want."[3]

The discovery of great numbers of poor people in America took many citizens by surprise. The country was, after all, the wealthiest that the world had ever known. It was a country of "affluence," one in which there seemed to be more than enough for all. As far as these citizens could see, there were already surpluses, and production was increasing every year. It was true that they occasionally encountered a poor person, but not millions of men, women,

---

[2]Excerpted from Louisa R. Shotwell, *The Harvesters: The Story of the Migrant People.* Copyright © 1961 by Louisa R. Shotwell. Reprinted by permission of Doubleday & Company, Inc.
[3]Excerpted from Kenan Heise, *They Speak for Themselves.* (Chicago, Ill.: The Young Christian Workers, 1965).

and children. There were a few hundred, perhaps, but not millions! Not even thousands! Millions of people living in poverty couldn't really exist. Wouldn't they have been seen?

Author Michael Harrington provided an explanation for this apparent contradiction.[4] He reported that failure to see the poor was due to the fact that, though numerous, they had become isolated and invisible. He described two Americas. The first was a familiar place. It was a land of plenty and comfort; a land flowing with goods and services; a land in which people did not ask themselves, "How can I ever manage to get the things that I need?" but rather, "What do I want next?" The "Other America" was different. It was a place of want and despair. It was a land of poverty!

The amazing thing about all of this is not that poverty existed but that its existence was such a shock to so many people; not that a problem *was* discovered but that it *had to be* discovered.

Poverty became a popular topic after Mr. Kennedy's discovery and Mr. Harrington's book. In 1964 President Lyndon Johnson announced that the United States would wage a "War on Poverty." Forces were mobilized and programs adopted. Concern about poverty reached a peak in 1967 and 1968 when riots occurred in dozens of American cities, riots with their roots in feelings of destitution, discrimination, and despair.

Hope that poverty really could be ended led Dr. Martin Luther King, Jr., to plan a "Poor People's March on Washington" for the summer of 1968. Hundreds of thousands of poor Americans would converge on the capital and stay there in Resurrection City until Congress acted. In that spring Dr. King was killed and the magic was lost. The poor marched and sang and camped but seemed to gain resentment instead of results.

The war on poverty was fought and the United States government finally had to settle for a "peace without victory." In 1974, after the war had been concluded, a Boston mother of four could still express the hopelessness that comes with poverty: "I can't go nowhere because there's nothing left after the rent and food. Sometimes I feel like I just want to give up."[5]

A number of other programs were adopted in the first half of the decade of the 1970s after the end of the War on Poverty, some to provide food for the poor, some to provide money, and some to provide jobs.

All of these programs, from the Kennedy administration on, have been critized—some for trying to do too much, some for trying to do too little, and some for attempting to do the wrong things. There has been no agreement as to how a war on poverty should be fought, who should fight it, or even whether it should be fought at all.

Part of the controversy that has surrounded the various programs stems from some fundamental disagreements over the nature, extent, and causes of poverty in the United States. While all who looked into the subject agreed that there were some poor Americans, not all agreed that there were the 30 to 70

[4] In his book *The Other America: Poverty in the United States.* (New York, N.Y.: The Macmillan Company, 1962).
[5] *Newsweek,* March 4, 1974.

million "discovered" by Mr. Kennedy's supporters in 1960 or the minimum of 25 million identified in the 1970 census. Those who doubted that poverty was extensive pointed out that these numbers were arrived at by counting all people with incomes below a certain figure, for example, $4,140 for a family of four in 1971. Many people with family incomes below this arbitrary poverty line lived a pretty good life, they pointed out. Those who saw poverty as a major problem countered that the figure selected for the poverty line was really much too low and that millions with incomes above the line lived in destitution.

Other dissenters raised serious questions about the severity of poverty in America. They pointed out that with very few (if any) exceptions, being poor in America was not the same as being poor in India or Haiti or Africa. They argued that poverty in America was not absolute poverty, the kind in which people actually starved to death, but a relative kind of poverty. People had enough to live on; they just didn't have as much as others in the society. Poor people in America, they said, are frequently better off than people of average means in other countries on this globe. Presidential candidate Barry M. Goldwater noted in 1964 that: "As our production and income levels have moved up over a hundred years, our concepts of what is poor have moved up also— and they always will! It is like greyhounds chasing a mechanical hare. You can never catch up. There will always be a lowest one-third or one-fifth"[6]

Just how much poverty is there in the United States? Where are the poor people to be found? How serious a problem is it? Is it also a problem for the affluent in America? For the nation as a whole? Is it possible to estimate how much it would cost the country to eliminate poverty? Can we estimate the cost of not eliminating it? Unless we can answer such questions, any kind of intelligent action is impossible.

There are poor people in America whether they number in the tens of millions or only in the hundreds of thousands and whether their poverty involves absolute misery or merely relative discomfort. What causes poverty? The problem cannot be dealt with until we have at least some answers to this question. Taxpayers will not be willing to support programs designed to improve the lives of the poor unless they believe that they have a responsibility to do so. If antipoverty programs are to succeed they must attack the roots of the problem. Why are poor people poor? Is it due to laziness? To lack of intelligence? Could they stop being poor if they were only willing to make the effort? Are they perhaps merely people who were unlucky enough to be in the wrong place or possess the wrong skills at the wrong time? Are they casualties of the industrialization of the country? Or might they be the unintentional victims of measures which were designed to help them but which backfired? Could it be that they are poor because of discrimination practiced against them by other individuals or groups?

By the middle of the 1970s a new dimension of the problem had appeared:

[6]From a speech given before the Economic Club of New York, quoted in *Vital Speeches,* Vol. 30, February 1, 1964.

The United States was hit by an energy crisis, inflation, and stiff competition from other nations for the limited resources of the world. The question became, would poverty be eliminated for all, or would all have to learn to accept scarcity? One writer predicted:

> Our awakening from the pleasant dream of infinite progress and the abolition of scarcity will be extremely painful. Institutionally, scarcity demands that we sooner or later achieve a full-fledged "steady-state" or "spaceman" economy. Thereafter, we shall have to live off the annual income the earth receives from the sun, and this means a forced end to our kind of abnormal affluence and an abrupt return to frugality.[7]

What are the implications of any such end of the era of affluence for poor Americans? If scarcity does return, will it mean even stiffer competition for limited goods and nothing at all left for the losers, or will it lead to a new set of values which will help end the present situation of poverty existing next to affluence?

There are many difficult questions to answer, but then, if the problem of poverty were a simple one, it would have been solved long ago. Among the important questions are these:

1. What do we mean by "poverty"? Is the problem of poverty in the United States today really serious enough to necessitate a "war"? If so, why was this problem not "discovered" until 1960?
2. Why are people poor? Is it anyone's fault?
3. How much poverty exists? Who are the poor?
4. What effects does poverty have on the people in the society who are not poor? On the society as a whole?
5. How can we deal with the problem of poverty? What kinds of solutions are available? What side effects must be guarded against when attempting to alleviate poverty and eliminate its causes?
6. Might the real danger be that it will be affluence rather than poverty that will be eliminated from America?

The chapters which follow will provide information that will help you come to your own conclusions about these questions.

[7]William Ophuls, "The Scarcity Society," *Harper's,* Vol. 248, April 1974.

2
IS THERE ANYTHING NEW ABOUT POVERTY?

An immigrant family.

"There is an ugly smell rising from the basement of the stately American Mansion."[1]

Poverty is certainly nothing new. Man has had to contend with it throughout his history. If the human race has somehow managed to survive thus far in spite of all this poverty, is there any special reason to be concerned about it now? If anything, there is less poverty today than there has been in the past. Is there something new about it now that makes it an urgent problem? Or is there something new about American society today that makes the presence of poverty more intolerable than it was in the past?

There is something new about American society today, for America has performed an economic miracle. With a population that exceeds 200 million, this nation has managed to create factories and farms so productive that they are able to provide not only enough for all but plenty for all. The average American today is able to consume quantities and varieties of goods and services that were beyond the grasp of even the most wealthy of previous centuries.

It is not necessary to go too far back in history (or too far from the shores of the United States) to learn of countries in which only a favored few could write their names or read the books that were available. In America today the young person who has not attended high school is looked upon with suspicion, and efforts are made to get everyone into college. Instead of having difficulty finding materials to read, as was the case in the past, the average American finds that he cannot keep up with all that is thrust upon him.

Just a short while ago only the wealthy could afford professional entertainment at frequent intervals. Today's American of modest means has but to turn a dial to be able to choose from among several kinds of performances. He may complain that it isn't all morally elevating, but he cannot complain that it isn't available.

Just a short while ago only the prosperous could afford to own a means of transportation capable of moving along at a speed of 10 or 15 miles an hour. Today it is assumed that the average man will own at least one automobile.

[1]Gunnar Myrdal, *Challenge to Affluence* (New York, N. Y.: Random House, 1963).

In addition, jet transportation is available whenever 70 miles an hour on the highway seems unbearably slow.

Many parents in times past found themselves hardpressed to provide complete sets of clothes, including shoes, for their children. More and more children today are embarrassed if they have to wear the same articles of apparel to school twice within the same week.

One shortage, it is true, still exists—that of housing. Even this shortage, however, is a sign of a society of plenty, for it comes less from a failure to build new homes than from an increase in family units. Grandparents, parents, and children used to share a house. Today each generation expects a place of its own.

In the past, men dreamed about cornucopias and talked about Gardens of Eden, but their real life was one of scarcity. Certainly there were periods in history in which there was plenty for some. Great powers, from the Assyrians and Babylonians of ancient times through the Incas of Peru to the colonial powers of the nineteenth and twentieth centuries, tried to gain plenty for their own people by conquering and exploiting other lands. There was plenty for the rulers, but not for the ruled. Other peoples, such as the citizens of ancient Athens and the plantation owners of the Old South, managed to achieve plenty for themselves by using the labor of slaves or serfs. There was plenty for the masters, but not for the slaves.

Enough for some but not for all; this has been the story throughout history. People had accepted the Biblical idea, "For ye have the poor with you always. . . ."[2] And then, suddenly, in the middle of the twentieth century, it appeared that "always" had ended. A new way of life with plenty for all had begun—or so many thought. John Kenneth Galbraith provided a popular name for this way of life when he titled his book *The Affluent Society.* Poverty in America today is different from poverty in previous ages because it exists within the context of this affluent society.

The Growth of a Land of Plenty

Rich human and material resources, hard work, and opportunity created this affluent society.

Millions of immigrants came to America because they saw here an unlimited potential. One historian has suggested that this potential for plenty is the key to understanding American character and institutions.[3] Americans never felt it necessary to have the government own and divide all the wealth or to establish rigid social classes to determine how the wealth would be divided. Why? Because they believed that there would be enough goods and opportunities for all. In other countries an individual could have comfort and plenty only if he took from others and left them in want. America with its seemingly

---

[2]Mark 14:7.
[3]David Potter, in his book *People of Plenty: Economic Abundance and the American Character* (Chicago, Ill.: University of Chicago Press, 1954).

unlimited resources suggested the possibility of a society in which each individual could have all he needed without depriving anyone else of his rightful share. Slavery was, of course, an exception to this, one that can be most generously explained by saying that it existed because it was the potential and not the reality that was unlimited at that time.

Those who came to America found a land rich in resources. The fertile lands of the central and southern sections of the Atlantic coast made agriculture profitable during the colonial period. In many of the colonies this agricultural prosperity was based on the labor of indentured servants and slaves brought by force from Africa. The Atlantic Ocean fostered fishing and commerce in the New England colonies. Farming, fishing, and commerce provided a base on which American prosperity could be built, though they could not, by themselves, create a land of plenty for all.

In the early nineteenth century textile mills and other factories became more and more common in the United States. Production climbed rapidly, and a growing prosperity attracted immigrants by the hundreds of thousands to American shores. These immigrants contributed to the growth of America, building the railroads which spanned the continent and manning the factories which turned out ever-increasing quantities of goods. These immigrants, however, although they were often better off than they had been in their native lands, seldom enjoyed plenty. Although wages for unskilled workers were higher in America than in Europe and the Orient, prices were higher too. The steady flow of new workers into the country and obstacles which prevented the formation of strong unions made it difficult for workers to bargain for a larger share of the profits of production.

In the late nineteenth and early twentieth centuries the increases in production were more dramatic than ever. The invention of mechanical harvesters and planters and the development of scientific farming methods made it possible for American farmers to produce more than the nation seemed able to consume. The formation of giant corporations and the development of mass production methods made it appear that production could outrun need. There was a financial panic in 1893, and the economy turned downward temporarily between 1900 and 1910, but these were just minor exceptions to the rule of steadily growing production and consumption.

Even the Great Depression of the 1930s did not shake this faith in America's ability to produce enough and to spare. True, the nature and severity of the Great Depression did lead some experts to believe that the United States' economy had become stagnant. They argued that all of the basic products that man needed for the good life had already been invented and produced and that from now on the country would have trouble finding people who could use the tremendous numbers of products that her farms and factories could turn out.

World War II helped to show that they were wrong, as it provided a temporary demand for all of the goods that could possibly be produced. American factories showed that they were able to turn out just about as many consumer goods as they had been able to while the country was at peace and,

at the same time, enough weapons and ammunition to bring the largest scale war in human history to a successful conclusion. The productive capacity of America had, indeed, become amazing. Furthermore, technology was providing even more efficient ways of increasing production every day. There appeared to be nothing that the economy could not accomplish. The average standard of living in America had gone up and up, and the percentage of people who could be classed as poor had gone down and down. There were still a few people who lived in want, but it seemed as if it would be just a matter of time until they too would enjoy the full benefits of the affluent society, the society which produced such a torrential flow of goods that its chief problem was getting rid of all that it had rather than figuring out how more could be produced.

This is not to say that everyone in the middle of the twentieth century was satisfied. As production and consumption had increased, so had desire. Mr. Smith could not be satisfied unless he kept up with, or perhaps was able to get ahead of, the Joneses. But the Joneses had more now than they had ever had before. The symbol of the affluent society was not the man who had plenty and was satisfied. It was, rather, the man who had plenty and felt that it was only natural to expect to have more.

Poverty Becomes "Invisible"

Under these conditions, the typical resident of suburban America did not give much thought to the question of poverty. Certainly few high school and college students from middle-class backgrounds talked about or even considered the possibility of a career dedicated to the elimination of poverty. Critics of the young people of the 1950s, indeed, often accused them of being too eager to get jobs in "big business," jobs that would ensure them steady employment until it was time to retire, a generous pension provision, and perhaps even a company-supplied burial plot upon death. Many seemed to feel that it was foolish to take economic risks to make gains for themselves, and unnecessary to sacrifice themselves by taking low-paying social service jobs to help others. The economy would provide plenty for all without risk or sacrifice.

Such an attitude was understandable. Conditions had just recently returned to normal following the Depression and World War II, and the poor had not yet become very vocal in their demands. Many Americans who were better off, in fact, could ignore poverty because they did not see it or hear of it. This had not been the case during the Great Depression. In the 1930s, poverty was everywhere. In the great cities there were men on street corners selling apples. In the parks, frequented at times by those fortunate enough to still have jobs, were "Hoovervilles" of tarpaper shacks thrown up by the unemployed. The suburban housewife, especially if her home was near a railroad or main highway, was frequently interrupted by knocks at the rear door which told her that another member of the army of unemployed, men forced to abandon their homes and families and wander about the country, was seeking odd jobs or a handout of food. In rural areas farms on which mortgages had been foreclosed or which had just been abandoned were common. Throughout the land newspapers and radio broadcasts emphasized the severity of the Depression and described the unemployment and poverty that it had brought in its wake. The government, under the New Deal, made deliberate efforts to bring information about the Depression to the people. Franklin D. Roosevelt, in his "Fireside Chats," tried to present the picture of the Depres-

Table 1 Unemployment in the United States

Year	Average Number of Workers Unemployed	Percent of the Total Civilian Labor Force
1900	1,420,000	5.0
1910	2,150,000	5.9
1920	1,670,000	4.0
1925	1,800,000	4.0
1930	4,340,000	8.7
1932	12,060,000	23.6
1934	11,340,000	21.7
1936	9,030,000	16.9
1938	10,390,000	19.0
1940	8,120,000	14.6
1945	1,040,000	1.9
1950	3,142,000	5.0
1955	2,654,000	4.0
1960	3,931,000	5.6
1965	3,456,000	4.6
1970	5,200,000	6.3
1973	5,400,000	6.0
1975	6,028,000	7.8

sion as a common problem of all Americans. He called on all to join in a common effort to end it.

The Depression hit all towns and cities and millions of families. The unemployment rates during the 1930s shown in Table 1 show how pervasive the problem was during that decade, especially when compared with the figures for the years before and since.

It wasn't easy to ignore poverty during those Depression years, but it was easy to ignore it in the 1950s. By the end of World War II poverty was no longer distributed evenly across the country. It had become concentrated in pockets which were frequently hidden away. The families of the comfortable had moved from the cities with their slum areas into the suburbs. True enough, the breadwinner who commuted into the city to work might encounter an occasional panhandler asking for a dime or quarter, but such panhandlers appeared more as evidences of human weakness than as symptoms of a widespread social problem. They could be dismissed as individuals lacking in strength of character who couldn't make their way in a society of opportunity and so had turned to alcohol instead.

Even the trip into the city on the railroad, a trip which usually took the commuter through the older and poorer sections of the city, began in the 1950s to be abandoned by the great majority of commuters. Freeways, parkways, and thruways, on which he alternately raced and crawled, took the commuter from suburb to office without the need or opportunity for a glance at the poor or their homes. His wife, in the meantime, had given up shopping trips into the city in favor of more convenient excursions to a suburban shopping center. Television even made it unnecessary for those desiring a wide choice of entertainment to travel into the city to find it.

Just about every community had its block of poorer homes tucked in behind the downtown stores or along the railroad tracks, but they were out of the way. Poverty, it appeared, was less of a problem than was crabgrass in the suburbs.

Rural poverty could also be ignored. Americans who wanted to get back to nature and see the farms could travel to the large areas of fine farm land where giant farms, often corporately owned, showed prosperity. To reach vacation lands, it was no longer necessary to follow slow roads through poor hill country areas or regions where men farmed sandy marginal soil. The same superhighways that took men into the cities took families to the mountains or seashores through often monotonous but seldom disturbing surroundings. As John Steinbeck wrote in *Travels with Charley,* "When we get these thruways across the whole country, as we will and must, it will be possible to drive from New York to California without seeing a single thing."[4] Even if the superhighway did not yet make it possible to travel anywhere in the United States without seeing poverty in the 1950s, the airplane did. Indeed, the supersonic transport will make it possible to travel from New York to California without seeing anything but selected short subjects (or perhaps an occasional travelogue if passengers express an interest in knowing what the country over which they are flying is like).

The Increased Visibility of Poverty

If it had just been a matter of growing suburbs and more rapid transportation, it should have been easier to ignore poverty in the 1960s than it had been in the preceding decade. But in the 1960s attention was focused on it to the extent that a war, even if not an all-out war, was waged against it. Why did poverty suddenly become a cause of national concern? Why, also, has that concern declined since the beginning of the 1970s?

One reason for the sudden attention to poverty was the "profit" orientation of the American political parties and communication media. John Kennedy's success in gaining first the nomination of the Democratic Party and then election to the Presidency in 1960 after taking a stand against poverty led others to call attention to the same issue. Newspapers, magazines, and broadcasting networks recognized the possibility of large audiences for material on the subject. This does not mean that the politicians, editors, and producers were insincere in their efforts to call attention to the problem or in their demands for reform. Once the public is interested, profit reinforces concern. Expressions of concern then become more public and more frequent. These expressions of concern in turn stimulate greater public interest in the subject, and it becomes a topic of national debate.

A second reason for the growing awareness of poverty was the change that had taken place in the attitude of the poor themselves. From the early days of the Puritan settlement of New England through the laissez-/faire period of the nineteenth century, poverty had been looked upon as a sign of inferiority

---

[4]John Steinbeck, *Travels with Charley.* (New York, N.Y.: The Viking Press, Inc., 1962).

by those who were better off but also by a large percentage of the poor themselves. The poor were so because they were sinful or unfit or lazy. Since poverty was regarded as a sign of such an undeserving state, no one could claim that he had a right to a better economic position. Improvement could come about by an individual's showing that he was deserving through hard work or cleverness or from a gift of charity for which he was expected to be appropriately grateful. This attitude has undergone considerable change in recent years. More and more people, especially the poor themselves but also many who are not living in poverty, have come to look upon want not as a sign of individual inferiority but as a social illness which must be cured by the entire society. Conversely, they have come to look upon an adequate standard of living not as evidence of the virtue of the few but as the right of all Americans.

What caused this change in attitude? Partly it was a result of the growth in size and complexity of the society. To the man in the city slum, surrounded by hundreds of thousands of others who are also badly off and isolated from those with adequate incomes who have moved from the city to the suburbs for a "better life," it is hard to see poverty as an individual condition. Partly it is the result of changes in industry. Many of the jobs that were traditionally used by hardworking but unskilled men as steppingstones toward a higher standard of living have disappeared. When these jobs were plentiful, an able-bodied man who was unemployed was likely to accept the idea that he had no one to blame but himself. As the jobs became scarcer and the man looking for work found none, he became more and more likely to blame society rather than himself for his condition.

Mass media, especially TV, also helped bring about this change in attitude. Adventure stories, family programs, and comedy hours all showed Americans living the affluent life. This affluence was not presented as something unusual but rather as the "normal" way in which Americans lived. Program after program presenting such a picture was interrupted only by commercials describing products which "everybody needs, deserves, and can easily afford." The poor were, in a sense, hit over the head with the idea that they were not sharing in the "normal" way of life which everyone "deserved." It should not have been surprising that many wanted their share.

The same change in attitude among the rural poor could also be traced to improved knowledge about what life was really like in the cities. Although there was still a steady flow of people from the farms to the cities in the 1960s, there was less of a tendency to look upon the latter as the "Promised Land" where all problems would automatically be solved.

A third reason for the rediscovery of poverty in the years after 1960 was the relationship between poverty and the problems of discrimination and race relationships. Some Americans argued that racism was the real problem and that poverty was just one of its results. Others argued that poverty was the real problem and that discrimination resulted from it. According to this second view, as long as there was not enough to go around, members of the majority group would rig the society in such a way that they would be assured of all they needed. Many members of minority groups would have to do without and the habits of poverty they developed would be used to justify continuation of the rigging.

Whichever argument was true, it became clear in the 1960s that poverty and discrimination could not be separated and that together they made an explosive mixture.

The seriousness of these problems had not been acknowledged in the 1950s. Poverty and discrimination then led only to peaceful protests and demonstrations and to a slow rise in the tax rate as the costs of welfare payments increased. Demands for new programs that would cause dramatic increases in taxes brought some attention to the problem in the early 1960s. But it was the series of riots which began in cities like Birmingham, Alabama, which spread to Chicago, Illinois, in 1963, and which became more serious in the Watts section of Los Angeles in the summer of 1965, that really awakened America. Looking at the destruction in Watts in 1965, some Americans feared that an insurrection might come. By the summer of 1967 many were convinced that the country was already in the middle of a full-scale revolution.

The War on Poverty of President Lyndon Johnson became popular, and new programs were adopted all across the country. Poverty was clearly a priority national issue through 1968 and 1969.

And then concern about poverty, or at least public attention to it, began to decline. Why?

One reason, certainly, was that the poor, who had hoped to achieve so much from either the governmental programs or from acts of violence, became disillusioned. The results did not match the promises, and many came to doubt that they justified the efforts. A few decided that it was much easier to cheat the system than to reform it and found ways of getting more from welfare than they were entitled to receive. Some became involved in the spreading drug scene and in the crime that was needed to support an expensive habit. Others just gave up. Many continued their efforts, but they could no longer attract as much attention.

When disillusionment set in and the riots quieted down, mainstream American concern also declined. Popular enthusiasm for a cause does not last long unless it is continually stimulated. Protests had been stimulants, and so had pronouncements from Washington. By 1970 the loud introduction of new programs by the Johnson Administration had been replaced by the quiet dismantling of those programs by the Nixon Administration.

There were also distractions. Much of the energy that had gone into the beginnings of the war on poverty were refocused into the anti-Vietnam War movement. The war concern gradually gave way to the environmental concern and then the energy crisis and Watergate[5] concerns. There were other crusades worth waging, and poverty lost its prominence.

[5]The break-in at Democratic headquarters in the Watergate building complex that led eventually to President Nixon's resignation in August 1974, and to the criminal convictions of many of his staff.

Finally, the nation entered into a period of new economic problems. The following sketch helps to explain why many stopped thinking about the finances of the poor and started to think about their own condition.

When Larry Hatley came home from the U.S. Army nine years ago, southern California was booming, and its aerospace industry was fat with orders from the airlines, the space agency and the Defense Department. He and his wife of four months, Pat, rented a large furnished apartment in North Hollywood for $110 a month, Larry picked up a well-/paid blue-collar job as an apprentice electrical-maintainance technician at Lockheed Aircraft, and the newlyweds started to live what they blissfully believed would be the middle-class American dream.

Larry bowled nearly every week night, and weekends were brightened by drive-in movies and dinners at a lobster house. By 1968, the Hatleys purchased their first real status symbol: an air-conditioned Pontiac Le-Mans. Larry successfully completed his apprenticeship. Their son Scott was born. In January 1970, they moved into a four-/bedroom, $24,000 house in suburban Simi Valley and also bought an expensive pedigreed dachshund.

It has been downhill since. Once strictly cash customers, the Hatleys picked up the credit-card habit—Master Charge, Montgomery Ward and J.C. Penney, to name a few—and soon became prisoners of the payment plan. Lockheed got into trouble, and as a result so did Larry. His $16,000 annual income fell to $14,000—and the good life started to go. First there were fewer bowling nights and an end to the lobster dinner—and finally, the painful sale of the Pontiac LeMans.

Then came the steady rise in prices. "Inflation just knocked me out of the box," Larry Hatley mournfully told *Newsweek's* Peter Greenberg last week. Last December, the Hatleys were forced to sell their dream house and find cheaper quarters in North Hollywood; they even gave away their dog. While Larry is making $6.50 an hour, he says that the escalating cost of living has forced him and Pat to cut the family food budget from $45 to $25 a week. Instead of the LeMans, the family has a used Volkswagen, and Hatley drives a Honda motorcycle to work. "We haven't been to a movie in over a year," he says. "I'm getting more and more over my head, and it's getting to the point where inflation is going to force me to send my wife back to work or I'll have to get a second job."

Saving: The Hatley dinner menu now offers a succession of hamburgers, hot dogs and luncheon meat and Larry no longer eats breakfast or lunch. "Too expensive," he says. "In the past," Pat Hatley says, "I never thought twice about throwing away small amounts of leftovers, but I'm not using the garbage disposal any more for food. I'm saving everything I can and I'm always on the prowl for new casserole recipes." Larry and Pat have also put off plans for another baby. "I'd like to have another kid," Larry said, "but doctor bills and delivery fees have skyrocketed. I can barely feed Scott."[6]

Interest in poverty was awakened in the 1960s and, although diminished, is still considerable. Some still see it as one of the greatest challenges to American society. Others view it as a minor problem that has been blown up out of all proportion. Those who see it as a great challenge are convinced that:

1. Poverty is no respecter of persons or places; it can strike any individual or group anywhere in the country.
2. There are tens of millions of people suffering from poverty throughout the country. Some of them are actually dying of starvation in an America that could easily afford to take proper care of them if it wished to do so.
3. Although the majority of those classed as poor in modern America may be better off than hundreds of millions of others around the world, their poverty is real and painful because it is in such marked contrast with the way of life of those in the mainstream of American affluence.
4. Poverty affects all Americans, not just those who are poor. It presents dangers to the economic prosperity, moral well-being, and physical security of the country.
5. If we are heading toward a period when sacrifices are going to be demanded, it is important to see that the poor who lack political power are not called upon to bear an unfair portion of the burden.

Those who feel that the problem is being exaggerated counter that:

1. Poverty is a personal rather than a national problem because it affects only certain kinds of people who lack the strength to overcome it.
2. The estimates of the number of poor are far too high because they are based on dollar incomes. There are opportunities available to all so that there is no excuse for anyone's starving in America.
3. There will always be a lowest one-fifth or one-quarter of the population, no matter how well off they are, so the concern should be with their actual rather than relative standard of living.
4. Poverty is not the cause of, but only an excuse for, the rioting and other dangers that have beset the nation.
5. We have enough to worry about now trying to lick inflation and compete for the world's resources. We need programs that will make us as efficient as possible, not ones which will help those who are inefficient.

Certainly there is no general agreement either as to the problem or the remedy. There is, however, need to search for answers to questions which will influence the quality of life Americans will lead in the future.

[6]"Blue Collar: Back to a VW," copyright © Newsweek, Inc., 1974; reprinted by permission.

What Do You Think?

1. Will the United States ever be able to increase production enough so that everyone can have all that he wants, or will people always want more than they have?

2. If you had to be poor, would you rather have most of the people around you poor also or better off? Why?

3 Does a country that is capable of producing plenty for all have a greater moral responsibility to fight poverty than a country that is not capable of doing so? Explain your reasoning.

4. What other factors besides those mentioned in the chapter help to explain why Americans have been more concerned about poverty during some decades than others?

ACTIVITIES FOR INVOLVEMENT

1. Write a description of the standard of living of an "average" American in the early colonial, Revolutionary, or Jacksonian period based on American history sources. Consider such things as food, clothing, shelter, transportation, entertainment, education, and governmental services. Then tell whether or not you would consider him poor and why.

2. Interview three or four adults who remember the Great Depression of the 1930s. Find out how it affected them personally. Write a report on the effects of the Depression on individuals based on your interviews.

3. There are a number of general statements concerning attitudes in the 1950s in this chapter. Ask your parents or other adults what they remember about this period and what their attitudes were then. How do they feel now about the period? Compare and contrast their answers with the general statements in the chapter. How would you explain the similarities and differences?

4. Conduct a poll among students outside your class and then among a sample of adults in your community as to whether or not they believe poverty is a serious problem in the United States today. Total the positive and negative responses which each group gives. How do the totals compare? How would you explain this?

5. Write a sketch similar to the one about the blue-collar worker telling how recent changes in the economy have helped or hurt a family's standard of living.

3
BEING POOR IN AN AFFLUENT SOCIETY

The problems of absolute poverty are easy to understand. The bony legs and arms, the distended stomach, and the haunted eyes of the child who is starving to death, whether on the main street of a city in India or hidden away in some corner of America, are easily recognized. There *are* people who suffer from such absolute poverty in the United States. The problems of the great majority of the poor in this affluent society, however, are much less easily comprehended. With either low-paying jobs or welfare funds available to them, most of the American poor do not display the traditional signs of total poverty: malnutrition and nakedness. They consume enough calories to appear well-fed, have enough clothing to appear "normal," and they may even have a television set in the home. If the home itself is cramped, cold, and bare, it is probably also located somewhere out of the sight of most Americans.

If the poor in the American affluent society are so much better off than millions in Asia, Africa, and Latin America, why aren't they satisfied? Are there special problems that add to the miseries of poverty when it exists in the midst of a society of plenty?

One answer to this is, "No." Those who give this answer argue that there will always be a poorest group in any society, no matter how wealthy it may be, and that poor people who don't have the ability or ambition to rise up in the society should just be thankful that they live in a country that can take care of all so that they are not starving.

Others argue that if the American poor lived their lives in a vacuum many of them might easily be contented but that modern technology abhors such vacuums. Radios and TV sets and means of rapid travel guarantee that the poor will be aware of the standard of living and of the expectations of the more affluent Americans. Even in times of inflation and concern about the supply of resources, commercials still tell of products that everyone needs, deserves, and can easily afford. Automobile commercials assume that every family should have at least one car; the only question is whether the listener should be content with an economy model or is one whose needs and taste for luxury entitle him to a "full-size" car.

In America, the poor are encouraged to feel the need for products they cannot afford. TV programs present as a normal way of life freedom of choice of occupation, place of residence, and associates. The poor feel themselves trapped. Public service announcements point the way to a better future. "To get a good job, get a good education." The realities of educational opportunities in poor and ghetto areas do not match the ideal. Schools for the poor all too often offer little if any hope to those who attend them.

The readings and pictures in this chapter show people who are hungry, people who have enough to meet their basic needs but nothing else, and people who are poor only in comparison with America's affluent majority. What is being "poor" like? Should all of these people be described as living in poverty?

1. Poverty in Appalachia

In the "hollows" or narrow valleys that stretch back into the hills in states like Kentucky and West Virginia are people who scratch a living from the soil or forests of the hillsides. Many of these families have lived in the same place for generations. The photo below shows the home of one of these families. The two men on the roof are the owner and an Associated Press reporter.

What Do You Think? ──────────────────────────

1. Which of the various modern conveniences that most Americans have do these people enjoy? What in the picture tells you this? Which of the conveniences do they probably lack? What in the picture tells you this?

2. What do you think is the most likely explanation of the automobiles being where they are in this picture?

3. How would a family living like this be most likely to earn their living?

21

2. "Lord, I'm Hungry"*

Some of the worst poverty areas in America are located in rich farming regions. One such region is the so-called Black Belt, which touches Arkansas and Louisiana on the west and Georgia on the east. It also includes large portions of Mississippi and Alabama. Long a center of cotton production, it is fertile land. A large percentage of the population is black.

The reading below describes conditions that have existed in the Mississippi Delta section of the Black Belt for the last 10 years.

Cleosa Henley just stood, a thick-shouldered, bullet-headed black ruin of 46, gazing dully out at the soybeans that have swallowed up his cotton rows, his garden patch and, very nearly, his life. Once, when cotton still was king in the Alabama Black Belt, it took 200 Negro tenant families to work Miss Nell Reed's plantation outside Boligee. Now, only a dozen remained in the surviving slapsided shacks, with little more than odd jobs or welfare to stave off starvation. Henley scratches up $30 a month loading timber when he's lucky, pays $10 a month rent for two cardboard-walled rooms and somehow stretches the rest into enough fatback, rice, grits, meal and greens to keep himself, his wife and seven kids alive. He can't remember the last time he ate meat, other than pig's ears, hog jowls or neck bones. Even relief costs money. Henley can buy $98 worth of Federal food stamps for $12—if he can ever put $12 together all at once. "I just ain't got that kinda money," says Henley, his gaze slowly dropping to his bare feet. "That money is right hard to git." . . .

He is often hungry, indeed, to the point of slow starvation—and [he has] become a national issue. [In April 1967] a Senate antipoverty subcommittee chaired by Pennsylvania's Joseph Clark . . . toured the flat, rich bottom lands of the Mississippi Delta—and came back appalled at the sight of Negro children with all the marks of malnutrition: bloated bellies, drowsy eyes, runny sores. . . .

Hunger is not, of course, a Mississippi monopoly. It can be found anywhere cotton grows, or once grew. A half-mile or so off the highway, the shacks begin in all their uniform squalor: the leaky roofs, the wood sides weathered raw and rotten, the flies droning in through glassless, screenless windows, the outdoor privy, and the indoor walls plastered over with so many layers of newspaper and flour paste that they look like papier-maché.

Faces: In one such shack, near Selma, Mrs. Florida Mae Andrew, 51, sits heavily in a rocker, starchy fat on a diet eked out of $20 a month for taking in washing, and sighs: "Lord, I'm so hungry I can't hardly stand up. But I got to go build a fire so's I can cook somethin'." In another, outside Greenville, Mississippi, hobbles Earl Jones—a shrunken, wrinkled man with a lame hip who is 36 and looks 50. He is one of the lucky ones: he takes home $20 a week

*Copyright © Newsweek, Inc., 1967; reprinted by permission.

as a tractor driver, a job not yet ground under by the new technology, and there is a pot of pinto beans simmering on the stove for dinner for his fourteen children. In still another shack, in Americus, Georgia, 12-year-old L. J. Crumbley, Jr., bubbles home from school with a spelling test he has just passed. The words—"meat," "soup," "lunch"—are abstractions: crippling rheumatism drove his father, an ex-sharecropper, off the land, and the family has no electricity, no water, no income, no hope. . . .

A good many Negroes do leave for the towns of the south or the ghettoes of the north. "Chicago, Chicago—that's all you hear," says an ex-farm worker in the delta. But others stay—and struggle for bare existence. Thousands of Negroes subsist on free Federal foods such as grits, rice, flour—an eggless, fruitless, tasteless dole that was never meant to do more than supplement a family's regular diet. "You eat corn bread and beans every day of your life and it weakens you down," an Alabama tenant farmer says accurately.

What Do You Think? _____

1. There is much talk about diet in this reading. Can a person's diet really affect his ability to earn a living? What evidence can you find to support your answer?
2. Twelve-year-old L. J. Crumbley, Jr., attends school. Is there anything in the article to indicate that education will lead to a better life for him? Explain.
3. How can the paradox of hunger existing in the midst of such rich farming land be explained?

_____

3. Welfare: The Starch Diet*

Life in the cities of the North is not always comfortable for the blacks of the Delta who make their way to them or for whites who have lived there for many years. In recent years, inflation has made things even worse.

Even in normal times, rations are short and life is grim for Mrs. Flora White and the four of her twelve children still living at home. They exist in a rundown four-bedroom tenement apartment in Boston's South End on approximately $216 a month from Federal welfare funds and another $220 in social-security payments, the only legacy of Mrs. White's husband, a parking-lot attendant who died of cancer seven years ago.

But now conditions are even worse. Before prices started to soar, Mrs. White says, "I used to be able to go to the store with $50 and come back with six or seven bags of groceries. Now I'm lucky if I come back with three." As a result, the White family diet is almost totally starch: government surplus macaroni and rice, canned spaghetti and frozen potpies, leavened by chicken and cold cuts "maybe every other night and fresh vegetables about twice a week," Mrs. White said.

Their rent is $214 a month, and that almost uses up the social-security check. "But that money belongs to the children," says Mrs. White. "Their father worked for it and left it to them, and the landlord shouldn't be able to take it away."

For pin money, the 50-year-old Mrs. White is permitted under government rules to baby-sit for a neighbor, a chore which nets her about $16 a week. But she has no social life at all. "I can't go nowhere because there's nothing left after the rent and food," she says. "Sometimes I feel like I just want to give up," Flora White told *Newsweek's* Sylvester Monroe, "but I have to think of the kids."

What Do You Think? _____

1. There are people in other parts of the world who are worse off than Mrs. White. Should she really be thought of as living in poverty?

2. How would you react to Mrs. White's statement that, "Their father worked for it [social security] and left it to them, and the landlord shouldn't be able to take it away."

4. Will the Pickers Come?*

Some of the poor live in the rural south and others in the urban north. There are still others who do not have permanent homes at all. These are the migrants. They are mostly farm workers who move around the country finding work wherever it is available and existing somehow when no work can be found. The following selection describes the homes and travels of typical migrant families.

Every spring the Fontanez family and other thousands fan out from the southwest in search of work in crops.

A minority of them migrate entirely inside the state they call home. There are a few states where, during every month of the year, one crop or another demands hand labor. A California migrant cycle may go from winter cotton to Imperial Valley vegetables, then on to San Joaquin apricots to peaches to beans to tomatoes to Fresno grapes, and meet itself again in fall and winter

*Excerpted from Louisa R. Shotwell, *The Harvesters: The Story of the Migrant People.* Copyright © 1961 by Louisa R. Shotwell. Reprinted by permission of Doubleday & Company, Inc.

cotton. Within Texas, cotton picking begins in July in the Rio Grande Valley and moves up the coast to central Texas; the harvest comes to a climax in the Panhandle in October and then dwindles through west Texas to a December end; meantime in the lower Rio Grande Valley and that fabulous sector that calls itself the Winter Garden there is vegetable and citrus harvest in winter and on through spring and early summer.

But most Spanish American migrants cross a score or more of state lines in the course of a crop season. Some start out from New Mexico or Arizona or California or Colorado. Those from Texas, where the greatest number have some kind of home base, are found during a single year working in thirty-two states.

Such are the hazards of weather, blight, market slumps, labor surplus, and time eaten up in travel and job hunting that if there exists a migrant who has found work for any fifty-two consecutive weeks, either within a single state or across the country, nobody has tracked him down.

Migrants may or may not return to home base for the winter. One Texas Mexican family turned up in the central New York State bean harvest four years after leaving the Texas community they still speak of as home. For some, home base is a house of their own somewhere across the tracks in the Mexican quarter of a southwestern town. Manuel Fontanez' wooden unpainted three rooms in the *colonia* of Crescent City was built by the family themselves on a thirty-foot square plot. To get the land they paid ten dollars down and a dollar a month whenever the man came around to collect. (Finally he stopped coming, and in time they heard he had moved to California.)

The house has in each room one glass window and one naked electric light bulb; it has an old-fashioned icebox only rarely containing ice but convenient for storing staples, an outdoor water faucet shared by half a dozen neighbors, a porch with two front doors, and a market value of eight hundred dollars. It does not trouble the Fontanezes that they have no deed to the property. They know it is theirs, and it does not occur to them that their possession of it may be threatened.

Some families consider their home a cabin in a distant migrant labor camp, the door padlocked against their return. For others the symbol of home is no more than the mental image of a camp where they have been before and to which they hope sometime to go back, with no padlock and no cabin designated in their own minds or anybody else's as theirs; everything they own in the world journeys with them as they follow the crops by truck or jalopy. Still others make no pretense at having a home base of any kind.

Some follow a familiar pattern from season to season, returning year after year to the same growers. Some, like the Fontanezes, travel in small immediate family groups; others move with families expanded by relatives of relatives to forty or fifty or seventy-five. Still others may be members of very much larger crews impersonally assembled afresh every season by labor contractors. More likely than not these never know by name or face the owner of the crop they are working in; they work not for Mr. Johnson or Mr. Brown or Mr. Van Leyden; they work in cherries or cotton or on the beans. Indeed, the odds are **25**

increasingly good that the owner is not a man at all but a corporation. Many Spanish Americans prefer the smaller groups. They set great store by their personal relationship with the farmer; the opportunity to identify themselves with his interests attracts them more than does work in a large-scale operation in which they feel no real sense of participation.

Unknown numbers set forth without a known destination, depending on roadside signs of "Tomato Pickers Wanted" or on newspaper displays asking for peach thinners or radio voices pleading for almond knockers. Or they count on that mystical instrument, the migrant grapevine, to tell them where sugar beets or broccoli or potatoes or carrots or lettuce may need extra hands for hoeing or thinning or harvesting.

The more knowledgeable among the family heads make contact with Farm Placement offices, affiliates of the United States Employment Service maintained in an attempt to perform the staggering role of mustering enough and not too many workers in the right place at the right time. Others shun these offices because Farm Placement personnel seem to smack of government authority and because they ask questions: in Latin-American minds questions from anybody in authority too often symbolize a prelude to jail. The Fontanezes share this fear of authority; they keep a healthy distance from employment offices. As a result, they have more than once had the disquieting experience of hearing that three hundred workers are needed in a particular crop, only to arrive there in company with droves of others like them to find that the three hundred jobs have been filled by workers recruited through employment service channels. Yet it takes more than half a dozen such incidents to dissipate their dread of formal face-to-face dealings with officials.

The eight-hundred-mile leg of the Fontanez journey to Missouri is a short one compared to some. The initial trek may carry them all the way to Idaho for potatoes, or to Wisconsin for asparagus or cherries, or to Michigan for sugar beets or blueberries. A good number of Texas Mexicans head first for Oregon, where laborers of Spanish American ancestry are welcomed for the early sugar beet and onion work because they are "accustomed to stoop labor and have for years engaged in this work." South Dakota acknowledges its indebtedness to them for the arduous weeding and thinning of 5300 acres of sugar beets, a harvest need that in this state lasts from mid-May to mid-July.

Some of the Latin crews (they prefer this euphemism, for they have learned from experience the opprobrium that attaches to the word "Mexican") make straight for the state of Washington, a northwest journey from south Texas upward of twenty-four hundred miles, where seasonal harvest needs extend from April to October and reach their peak in June. For this trip the customary departure time is three in the morning, allowing a day and a night to Las Cruces, New Mexico, another day and night across Arizona to Blyth, California, and a third twenty-four hour lap to carry them to Washington.

What Do You Think?

1. The man from whom the Fontanez family obtained its lot did not give them a deed and apparently just stopped collecting for it and moved to California. How can these actions be explained?
2. Is this need to be on the move all the time a sign of poverty? How else might you explain their constant travelling?
3. Can anyone who owns his own home be considered poor? Explain.
4. How would you explain the attitude toward people in authority which migrants display? Is there any relationship between this attitude and poverty? Explain.

5. Keeping House in a Hogan for a Family of 12*

A large number of American Indians are outside of the affluent mainstream of American society, some as a result of discrimination and others by choice. The following section was prepared as a description of a way of life for the "Family, Food, Fashion, and Furnishings" section of The New York Times, *not as a social*

*Martin Waldron, *The New York Times,* May 14, 1974. Copyright © 1974 by The New York Times Company. Reprinted by permission.

commentary. It can, therefore, be especially valuable to the reader who wishes to draw his own conclusions about what is and what is not poverty.

Whippoorwhill, Ariz.—Mrs. Alice B. Yazzie, a Navajo Indian, is 36 years old. She looks older.

Standing in the hut, 12 feet in diameter, where she lives on a remote Arizona mesa with her husband, Joe, and 10 children, she giggled like a teen-ager as she cooked fry bread for recent visitors.

She speaks no English. But she knows what a camera is: Before she would allow her picture to be taken, she demanded time to change from the revealing cotton ribbed T-shirt she was wearing to a traditional Navajo costume.

The Yazzies are said by tribal officials to be typical rural Navajos living off the land deep within the 25,000-square-mile Navajo reservation.

Although the land is bitter cold in winter and swelteringly hot in summer, the Yazzies do not find it an unpleasant life.

By any statistical standard, Alice Yazzie and her family would be considered underprivileged. Except for a few refinements—a cook stove, a truck, organized schools and a coin laundry 10 miles away—they live pretty much as Navajos have lived here for a thousand years.

Children Still at Home

The Yazzies' children range in age from 2 to 22 and all of them are still at home, living with their parents in the hogan, the traditional Navajo lodging of cedar logs and mud.

The Yazzies have no electricity, no telephone, no water. The nearest water is 10 miles away at a trading post along with the coin laundry. The Yazzies have no mail delivery and the Indian school where the children go is 35 miles away.

Mrs. Yazzie seems content. As she mixes and fries Navajo bread, she keeps a sparkling eye on her visitors and breaks into laughter as an interpreter makes a remark in Navajo.

"Poor? Underprivileged? What are those terms?" demanded the intermediary, Clare M. Thompson, who is an official interpreter for the Navajo Indian Tribal Council.

"They have the sun. They have space. They have fresh air," he said. "What is being poor is living in ghettos in New York City or Washington. They have polluted air. They have no sun. They have no place for the children to run and play.

The Yazzie children have room to run and play. As far as the eye can see, up to 75 miles, there is nothing but an occasional wolf and miles of scrubby sagebrush.

"Indians use sagebrush to treat colds," Mr. Thompson said, leaning down to wipe the nose of one of the Yazzie children and pinching of a sprig of sagebrush at the same time. "Smell this" (crushed, it smells like mentholatum).

How much money do the Yazzies have to live on? How do they spend it?

Such questions are considered impertinent by the proud and haughty Navajos, and when Mrs. Yazzie was asked, there was a long silence. She was too polite to indicate to the interpreter that she considered it to be a tasteless query.

Mr. Thompson would not explore further the finances of the Yazzies, but he did make an educated guess about a typical Navajo family who might be living, as the Yazzies do, 35 miles from the nearest town.

First, like the Yazzies, such a family would have a flock of 20 to 50 sheep, with income from the sheep approximating $1,200 a year.

A family with 10 children would get $185 to $200 a month from the Bureau of Indian Affairs, Mr. Thompson continued, and would be eligible for surplus farm products distributed by the Federal Government—beans, butter, rice, peanut butter, lard and flour.

With no rent or utility bills, this family would be able to pay $85 a month toward the cost of buying a pickup truck, he added.

Haul Water in Milk Cans

The Yazzies have such a truck. They use it to shop at the trading post 10 miles away and to haul milk cans filled with drinking water to the hogan.

Keeping house for a family of 12 is no overwhelming task in a hogan. The Yazzies have two beds. Four people sleep on them while the other eight family members sleep on sheepskins thrown on the earth floor at night. During the day the sheepskins are hung outside to air.

Cooking is done on a two-eye iron stove in the middle of the hogan. An exhaust pipe runs from the stove to the mud roof.

The staple of the Yazzie diet is fry bread.

The family eats one big meal a day—beans, rice and meat (lamb or mutton from the family flock, or pork or beef from the trading post).

Occasionally at the trading post, the Yazzies buy carrots, lettuce and other fresh vegetables, paying approximately twice as much for them as do families in the cities.

Mrs. Yazzie's fry bread recipe, as given by her daughter, Sarah, seems inadequate. "A handful of flour, a pinch of baking powder, some salt and some water," the 19-year-old girl explained.

The bread is cooked in melted lard. The lard is considered hot enough to cook the bread when a kitchen match floating in it catches fire.

To make a loaf, Mrs. Yazzie pinched off a fist-sized piece of dough and twirled it with her hands until it resembled a small pizza.

The bread is cooked in the sputtering lard until it is brown on both sides. It is surprisingly light and delicate.

Although the Yazzies are not regularly exposed to radio, television or newspapers, the influence of advertising has reached them. Mrs. Yazzie uses popular bleaches and detergents when she has her laundry done at the trading post.

Navajo families who live in the recesses of the reservation do little or no entertaining. They party by driving to a bar off the reservation (for those who want a drink at home, mobile bootleggers make regular rounds on the back trails, selling liquor illegally at extremely inflated prices).

When a member of the family is ill the Yazzies can drive 100 miles or so to the Navajo hospital at Window Rock, Ariz., or they can consult a medicine man nearby. Most Navajo medicine men are said to be combinations of herb doctors, natural psychiatrists and religious leaders.

Conjugality between husband and wife in a 12-foot hogan with 10 children would seem to be an impossibility, if one desired privacy.

"Not so," said Mr. Thompson with a glance at Mrs. Yazzie, who was making more fry bread. "Where there's a will there's a way."

What Do You Think? _____

1. What would you consider the chief advantages and disadvantages of the life that the Yazzies lead?
2. Why do you think Mrs. Yazzie was willing to discuss most other matters but considered questions about money to be impertinent?
3. Would you consider the Yazzies a "poverty" family?

6. Poverty in New York

According to Mr. Thompson, in the previous reading, to be poor is to live in New York City's crowded slums. The picture below is of such an area in the part of the city known as the South Bronx. During the late 1960s and early 1970s many of the owners of buildings in the area found that it was more profitable to abandon the buildings and take a tax loss than to try to maintain them and pay high city taxes.

What Do You Think?

1. What would be the main problems that would result from living in a building such as the one on the right in this picture?
2. If you were the owner of this building and found that you were losing money on it, what would you do?

---

7. Life on Welfare: A Daily Struggle for Existence*

Many of the families living in buildings in the poor areas of the cities are on welfare. The welfare departments in the big cities hire experts whose job it is to determine exactly what a family or an individual needs to maintain life in the city and how much these things cost. The number of razor blades needed per year by the employed man, the number of bars of soap needed per person per year, the amount of deodorant for an unemployed woman, all are computed and used to determine the amount to be paid to welfare clients. If absolute poverty is not the problem of the welfare client, then, what is? The next reading describes life on welfare in New York City.

It was 6:30 in the morning and the Pressley family—Ruth Pressley and her six children—started moving about their Harlem apartment in a swift, although sleepy-eyed, routine of getting ready for school.

An ancient radio, with an uncovered speaker, sputtered and buzzed as it gave out time signals, commercials, music and news.

"Get that big O.K. for cash today," a jingle blared on behalf of a loan company.

"It's 6:45, Ruthie," Mrs. Pressley called to her 16-year-old daughter, repeating a time check. "Come out of that bathroom."

Then in quick succession the radio listeners were urged to both "See the Dodge boys, today" and "Jet Delta to Birmingham" before another time signal was called.

"Sharon," Mrs. Pressley called to another daughter, "It's 6:54; is that oatmeal on?"

Mrs. Pressley, a 45-year-old, raw-boned, deliberate woman says she does not "hear" many of the morning commercials.

While some people screen out commercials by choice, the Pressleys do it out of necessity, out of defense. This family is on relief and like more than 655,000 of New York's poorest, they survive in the backwash of the city's mainstream.

Many goods and services considered normal for most people must be

---

*Thomas A. Johnson, *The New York Times,* December 19, 1966. Copyright © 1966 by The New York Times Company. Reprinted by permission.

31

acquired at a sacrifice for welfare recipients or forgotten. Two bus fares, for instance, or a package of cigarettes could take half of the daily food allotment of about 90 cents for a family member who eats at home. And a single person, authorized to eat in restaurants, could not buy a ticket to some first-run movies with his daily food grant of $2.50.

"I listen to some commercials about detergents," Mrs. Pressley told a visitor recently as she chased roaches from the breakfast table. "I want to see what they say about getting clothes clean."

While she washed the table, a cheery voice on the radio proclaimed: "Oh, yes, things are great in Ford country."

To observe public assistance from the recipients' point of view, this reporter for *The New York Times* lived recently with families on relief and also in a furnished room in a residence hotel that houses mostly single welfare clients.

Many clients, because of their age, an illness, lack of training, or discrimination, were found to have no hope for joining the more affluent majority.

Despair and cynicism shape much of their thinking.

For many, cheating "the system" has become a way of life, a survival technique.

For the Pressleys that morning's breakfast was simply oatmeal and tea. There have been times, Mrs. Pressley said, when the children had no breakfast at all.

Susan Pressley, who is 7 years old, said she would like some corn flakes for breakfast as she waited for an older sister, Mary, who is 11, to finish using a cereal bowl.

Mrs. Pressley promised to buy corn flakes ("not the sugared kind—they cost too much") when the welfare check arrived.

"That's one reason why I went to work," Mrs. Pressley explained "so I could have a little more money for my family. It's not much more, though, and it doesn't go very far when you add up the carfare and cleaning bills and such."

Before she went to work in July as a part-time neighborhood aide for the Urban League's Open City program that promotes housing desegration, Mrs. Pressley had received $184 twice a month from the Welfare Department. The department now deducts her weekly salary ($30) from the welfare allowance but adds employment expenses (carfare, lunch, clothes, cleaning bills, etc.) so that her combined income now comes to $203 twice a month.

"I also want the children to see me working, too—to see that life is more than waiting for a government check," she said.

In an informal accounting, Mrs. Pressley estimated that her monthly expenditures were: food, $150; rent, $111; clothing, $20; gas and electricity, $15; cost for care of her son, Christopher, 3, while she works, $52; employment expenses, $20; household supplies, $7; laundry, $7; personal items, $12; school expenses, $5 and roach killer, $4. The total: $403.

"We buy chickens a lot and pork roasts, fish, or stew beef—whatever is cheap on check day," Mrs. Pressley said. She said it was not possible to save for a movie. "There's never enough."

Mrs. Pressley came to New York from Roanoke, Va., in the early nineteen-forties. She worked as a streetcar conductor during World War II and later as a 35-cent-an-hour domestic and factory worker. Her first contact with the Welfare Department, she said, was about 16 years ago. Since then she has received public assistance "off and on," the last time starting about three years ago after a separation from her husband. He is disabled now, she said, and lives in Brooklyn, also on public assistance.

During the years, Mrs. Pressley said, she has not developed any particular pattern of dealing with case workers. "They change too often," she said. "By the time we get to know one another, the investigator's been changed."

Mrs. Pressley is suspicious of the whole welfare system, noting that millions of dollars are spent, but clients "receive so little."

"Somebody must be stealing like mad down there," she said half joking.

Mrs. Pressley said that in the past, when she tried to work while on welfare, things did not go smoothly.

"Once, I was working and I told the investigator not to call the employer and that I would show him my pay receipt as proof. He called my boss to check and I was fired the same day—many people don't want clients working for them."

Another time, Mrs. Pressley said she had worked as a nurse's aid for four months and her case worker failed to record the income. "Suddenly they closed my case and they said I was indicted for grand larceny for concealing my income, but the judge threw the case out of court."

"The case was closed for a long time and I got desperate," she said. "I put on a tight skirt and a lot of make-up and went to a bar on Lenox Avenue. But the bartender said: 'You're no prostitute, what're you doing here?' I told him, and he gave me a couple of dollars and told me to go to the police station the next day. The police gave me a box of food."

The Pressley household, where the children range from 3 to 16, does not have bicycles, toys, coloring books or comic books. It is, for the most part, a household of functional objects needed for a semblance of modern-day survival. But even these, the broken beds and dressers, the unmatched chairs and tables, have all served other households before.

But the furnishings are hardly Mrs. Pressley's biggest worry.

"He doesn't talk about it, but I know my son would like to go to the movies with his friends," she said. "And my daughters, they would like to be able to buy stylish clothes. They don't talk about these things but I know they would like to do them."

A visitor to the Pressley apartment steps into a long, dimly lit hallway, covered with dark green paint. Rust stains from broken water pipes show through the paint on the upper floors.

The apartment is kept very clean and despite a continuing battle against them, roaches climb the walls, walk the floors and invade dressers and closets.

"I guess we spend about a dollar a week on roach killer insecticides," Mrs. Pressley said, "but they always come back. They live in the walls and under the floors. They always come back."

Craig Pressley, who is 14, warned a visitor recently that a roach had crawled on top of the visitor's shoe. "Kill it," Craig said.

The visitor dislodged the insect but missed in a clumsy attempt to smash it. A young neighbor did the job, expertly, with his foot. . . .

[There are many people on public assistance or welfare who are even worse off.]

There are thousands of aged persons who live as frightened recluses in what are known as single room occupancy accommodations, many on the West Side. Here, however, a good percentage of the aged are white and were left alone when their children moved from the city to the suburbs. They spend much of their time waiting for visits from their children. When the weather is good they crowd the benches on Broadway's center mall. Welfare laws require children to support their parents if they are able to and some receive money from their children.

Since World II these elderly persons have been joined by thousands of disabled and low-salaried non-whites and in the poorer serviced "residence hotels," many live in their cell-like cubicles in constant and often justified fear of marauding drug addicts, drunks, and petty criminals.

Facilities at many of these buildings are dehumanizing at best. In many cases they are unhealthy and unsafe.

Kitchen and bathroom facilities in these buildings are shared.

One woman, disabled by a cardiac condition, said: "I used to clean up the bathroom every day, but then other people, nasty people from all the other floors, used to troop to this bathroom because it was clean. Then they would mess it up. I only clean for myself now."

Another woman said there were no locks on the bathroom doors and tenants sing or talk while using the facilities. Locks, she said, had been placed on the bathroom doors but visitors or addicts, who did not have keys, broke them.

The dehumanizing conditions in these buildings is matched, perhaps, only by the ability of landlords to utilize every inch of space. Thus, dumbwaiter shafts have been plugged and are used as closets. Closets have been converted into tiny kitchens. These kitchens hold a small refrigerator with a two-burner hotplate on top of the refrigerator. Completing the arrangement is a kitchen cabinet—an orange crate nailed to the wall.

Garbage receptacles consist of a large tin or cardboard drum (or sometimes just a burlap bag), in the hallway. But infrequent collection by the superintendent has a predictable result: a garbage strewn hallway, a condition that inevitably attracts rats.

"They are never emptied on the weekends," said one elderly relief client-pensioner, retired a few years ago after working for 40 years in the garment district. "On the weekends you can't even get to the stairs for the garbage on the floor."

"I keep my garbage inside my room at night if I forget to put it out earlier," said Mrs. Ursela Brazer, who receives public assistance for herself and her 7-year-old daughter at the Pendleton Hotel. . . .

Although such single room occupancy buildings are officially only supposed to have one person a room, many house women with children because it is difficult for the Welfare Department to find places for its clients.

A native of the Virgin Islands, Mrs. Brazer said most of the women tenants she knew opened their doors only during daylight hours. "Many bums walk in and out of the house," she said. "They often knock on the doors at night."

Other night sounds include the thud of garbage bags when they land in courtyards. Some tenants admit dispatching refuse "by air mail." They fear being mugged in dark or unlit hallways at night; they are afraid rats will crawl into their rooms if they keep garbage. . . .

But the major problem of the welfare recipient is living on the welfare grant.

A South Bronx mother complained: "You want to be the same as people who are not on relief, but you just can't do it. You never have enough money —I don't know what to do."

Another mother on welfare admitted finding a solution. Young and attractive, she walked recently along Columbus Avenue near 81st Street and in a low voice asked men if they were interested in "some sport." She admitted later to "tricking" in order to earn extra money. But, she explained, she never operated "close to where I live, or around people I know."

Another welfare recipient was not so circumspect. Asked by school officials why her children went to sleep in class, the mother said that sometimes she kept them outside the apartment until late at night.

"I have to do business if they're going to eat," she said.

While welfare budgets are computed to cover a variety of needs, most recipients say they can pay only the essential bills—rent, gas and electricity —while the remainder is spent for food.

A 48-year-old woman who came to the Lower East Side 10 years ago from Puerto Rico, and worked steadily until she was disabled by diabetes three years ago, finds that she often must depend on handouts from friends or live on bread and coffee.

Her twice monthly check is $35.40. Her rent is $23.40 a month. Gas and electricity costs about $17 every two months. The remainder is spent on food.

"There is never enough food for the full two weeks and never even enough for a pair of stockings," she said.

The woman said she had been given a winter coat by the Welfare Department but it was stolen and her case worker is so overworked she cannot take time to comply with the various departmental procedures required to have the garment replaced.

The recipient wears a neighbor's coat to visit the Lower Manhattan Welfare Center every few days to inquire about the replacement. She says she could not leave her house if her neighbor decided to go outdoors on the same day.

The checks that welfare recipients receive twice each month set in motion a predictable series of events.

35

It starts with the mailman.

Mailboxes in many slum buildings no longer protect their contents from theft. Long ago their locks were broken and their panels smashed. As a result, checks are either handed to waiting recipients or left with landlords or building superintendents.

Flanked by guards, many landlords sit inside barred rooms where they cash welfare checks and issue rent receipts.

Later, the salesmen arrive with thick account books and the ability to deliver almost anything a welfare recipient wants (for a signature). They hustle in and out of the buildings where recipients live collecting a payment here and selling a new item there. Their pattern, like that of many appliance and furniture stores selling goods on time to unemployed welfare recipients, is to collect as much of the debt as possible and repossess the item if payments stop.

While a few of the welfare recipients descend on supermarkets for provisions on check day, most hurry to small, neighborhood grocers. Prices are higher in the smaller stores, and there is less of a selection. But the neighborhood grocer extends credit during the lean days.

An assistant state attorney general said price gouging of welfare recipients —from overpriced appliances to supermarkets raising prices on check day— were "commercial facts of life."

"Most supermarkets will not admit it," said the state official, Joseph Bailey, "but some do raise their prices on check day. Some do it to offset the cost of hiring guards who patrol the stores against pilferage."

A spokesman for the New York State Retail Food Merchants Association denied such a pattern on the part of "reputable supermarkets."

"They're all competing for the dollar and will keep their prices as low as they can," the spokesman said.

The arrival of checks during the day also brings problems at night.

The police have noted that there is an upsurge of violent crimes on check night. They also think that many incidents probably go unreported.

"We get a lot of drunks rolled, a lot of pocketbooks and sometimes groceries snatched and some muggings," a Police Department spokesman said. "Many alkys (alcoholics) get taken over and over again."

Parties, or "check gigs," are sometimes thrown by recipients in celebration of their twice-monthly incomes. Questioned about a recent West Side "gig," the hostess said she liked the music, the drinks, and the people.

"Don't you give parties?" she asked.

What Do You Think? _____

1. Mrs. Pressley tells of things she knows her children want but do not talk about. Why don't they talk about them?

2. Would most of the problems of the welfare recipients be solved if they spent their check more wisely?

3. If you had to be on welfare, which of the following would bother you the most: shortage of food and clothing, doing without things you knew most Americans had, or the way other people look down on welfare clients.

4. What answer would you have given the welfare recipient who, when asked why she gave parties, responded by asking, "Don't you give parties?"

5. Does poverty endanger family life? Explain.

---

8. Welfare Hotel

Food prices and rent have risen sharply since the article on the Pressleys was written, but little else has changed. The following picture shows a welfare family temporarily housed in a hotel. At the time the picture was taken they had been in the temporary quarters for six months at a cost of $271 a month.

What Do You Think? _____

1. Should this family be considered fortunate or unfortunate to be living in this fashion in a hotel?

2. In what ways is this situation better than that of the Indian family living in the hogan? In what ways it it worse?

ACTIVITIES FOR INVOLVEMENT

1. Take an outline map of the United States and draw in the areas of poverty described in the sections in this chapter. As other areas are described in later chapters or in your research or class discussions, add them to the map.

2. Review all the selections included in this chapter. What evidence can you find to indicate that poverty is not restricted to any one section of the country, any one setting, or any one group of people? Write a "Letter to the Editor" responding to an editorial entitled, "All Poor People Are Alike."

3. Prepare a written research report on the history of a specific area of poverty. Your paper should include such things as:
   a. The location and description of the area.
   b. A description of the people who live there.
   c. The economic history of the area: Has it always been poor?
   d. The causes of poverty in the area.
   e. What is being done and what can be done to overcome poverty.

4. Listen to a morning "time, music, and news" type program for half an hour. List all the announcements and commercials that a family like the Pressley's would have to "screen out."

5. Make up a menu for a minimum balanced diet for a family of four for one day. Decide how much of different food products would be needed to provide adequate nutrition. Then, using either newspaper ads or actual market prices, figure out the cost of the food for your menu. Multiply by 30 to discover how much a family would need for food alone for a month.

6. Compare the lives of the different groups of poor people in this chapter. Which is worse—to be poor in the country or in the city? To have a miserable home or no home at all? Explain your reasoning.

7. If you had $1,000 you wished to give away, to which of the people described in this chapter would you give it? Defend your choice.

4
HOW MUCH
POVERTY EXISTS
IN AMERICA?

The election campaign of 1960, which brought attention to the issue of poverty, took place during a census year. Figures from the 1960 census were used in efforts to determine just how many poor people there were in America. Families with incomes below $3,000 per year and unattached individuals with incomes below $1,500 were classified as "poor." On the basis of the 1960 census figures the number of people in the United States living below these income levels was put at 35 million. This was nearly one-fifth of the total population.

The $3,000 and $1,500 figures used in interpreting the 1960 census were derived from a study made by the U.S. Department of Labor in 1959 concerning the amount of income needed for an adequate standard of living in the United States. Though the amount needed varied from place to place, it averaged about $6,000 for a family of four.

The $3,000 figure was chosen, therefore, because it was just half of the amount which people needed to maintain an adequate standard of living. Census readers described those families and individuals with incomes between the poverty line and the "adequate" line as "deprived." The deprived numbered about 30 million in 1960. Adding the number of deprived to the number of those living in poverty gave a figure of 65 million. This figure represented over one-third of the population in 1960.

There has been steady inflation in America since 1960, and the "poverty line" has been raised accordingly. By 1971, for example, the low-income line for a family of four was set at $4,140. Based on the 1970 count, the Bureau of the Census figured that there were about 26.5 million people in America living below that line in 1971, or about 12.5 percent of the total population.

Not everyone who is concerned about the question of poverty is willing to accept these census figures as an accurate reflection of the amount of poverty in America. Some object to the figures because they feel that they are much too low. These argue that the $3,000 figure was less than a family really needed in 1960 and that it hasn't been raised enough to counter inflation since. Most of those with incomes below about $7,000 should be counted as poor, they insist. Other experts object to the census figures because they think they assign too many people to the poverty category. These argue that low dollar income does not necessarily mean a low standard of living or hopeless poverty and that each case should be evaluated separately. They also argue that most of those with incomes under $4,140 seem to enjoy many of the items that are considered luxury goods in the rest of the world and, therefore, should not be considered poor.

The readings in this chapter provide a comparison between poverty in America and poverty elsewhere and then conflicting views about the actual amount of poverty in the United States.

1. The *Good* Side of the World

Americans have had economic and political problems in the 1970s. This cartoon by Pat Oliphant presents an interesting perspective on them. What is its point.

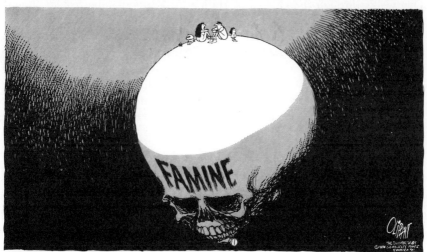

'UNEMPLOYMENT, INFLATION, HIGH FOOD PRICES, IMPOSSIBLE INTEREST RATES, BAD LEADERSHIP . . . AND THIS IS THE <u>GOOD</u> SIDE OF THE WORLD!'

Editorial cartoon by Pat Oliphant, copyright © the Denver *Post.* Reprinted with permission of Los Angeles Times Syndicate.

What Do You Think?

1. How valid is the idea of dividing the world between a "good side" and a "bad side"?
2. How real is the problem of famine in other lands?
3. Is it possible for people to live on the "good side" of the world and still have problems that are as serious as any of those on the "bad side"?

2. Viet Poverty*

Jeff Canning is News Editor of the Mamaroneck, New York, Daily Times. *While in the U.S. Army he learned the Vietnamese language and developed a strong feeling for the Vietnamese people. After direct American participation in the war had ceased, Mr. Canning went to Saigon to find out what things were really like. Among his findings were these about Vietnamese poverty, recorded shortly before Saigon fell to the communists.*

*Jeff Canning.

A lot is said about poverty in America. Most people generally agree it should be eliminated, and President Johnson even declared war on poverty a few years ago.

In America you're considered poor if, according to the charts, a certain number of people in a family don't bring home X thousands of dollars a year. One walks through the ghettos of Harlem or Watts or hundreds of similar places, looks at the debris in the streets and alleys, the housing that has seen better days, notes the leaky plumbing and says, "That's poverty."

Halfway around the world from this American poverty lies the teeming city of Saigon, capital of the embattled Republic of Viet Nam. Some two million people, many of them refugees from more than three decades of virtually uninterrupted warfare, are jammed into this metropolis on the banks of the Saigon River. The attractively landscaped government buildings and the broad boulevards of the international colony hold their own in comparison with western cities (if one mentally blots out the omnipresent barbed wire; life still revolves around the war). But these areas are only a small part of the city. Most of the people live in quote another Saigon—a Saigon of back alleys where the only open space near a dwelling is a few square feet of dusty (or muddy, depending on the season) alley pounded by an almost incessant procession of feet, bicycles and motorcycles; a Saigon of shantytowns where families slap sheets of tin and pieces of packing crates and cardboard together to keep out the monsoon rains and the burning sunshine as best they can.

Two weeks in Saigon taught this reporter more about poverty than all the literature he ever read on the subject.

One understands in Saigon what Dennis Bloodworth meant when he wrote in his book, *An Eye for the Dragon: Southeast Asia Observed, 1954–1970,* "The well-to-do West can afford inequality, because most of the poor can afford to be poor." Bloodworth, veteran Southeast Asian correspondent of the London Observer, reached that conclusion after taking his Hong Kong-born Chinese wife, at her request, on a tour of London's worst slums. Having heard a lot about western poverty, she was trying to find some that matched her Asian experiences, but later told her husband, "No. It's no good. You don't understand. I mean poor people, REALLY poor people." To which Bloodworth replied, "I'm sorry. These are the best I can find."

By American standards, most Saigonese live in indescribable poverty. But it doesn't seem to bother them. Being poor in Saigon doesn't carry a stigma the way it does in many parts of the West; there simply are too many people in the same sampan. There is no shame in sleeping in a doorway or on the sidewalk when one has plenty of company in all directions. A naked (or nearly so) youngster is not embarrassed to urinate or defecate in the gutter; for many, the gutter is the only lavatory they know.

Many residents of Saigon and other parts of South Viet Nam would qualify for all sorts of public assistance in the United States. The government of President Nguyen Van Thieu does run some programs, especially for orphans and refugees, but these efforts come nowhere near helping all those in need. So the needy must struggle to their own two feet and make do as best

they can. And they do, for the most part. They do manual labor. They pedal cyclos (three-wheeled vehicles resembling a bicycle with a lounge chair up front; some are motorized, but most are pedaled by the operator). They sell tickets for the national lottery. They sit on the sidewalks and hawk any goods they can acquire. Any sort of work, even if the day's yield is only a few hundred piastres (when this reporter was in Saigon in October 1973, 525 piastres equalled one U.S. dollar; inflation and devaluation have increased the ratio slightly since), the price of a decent meal.

The resiliency of Saigon's poor is remarkable. No matter how many times fate knocks them down, most Vietnamese of this reporter's acquaintance get right back up and try again. Most of the beggars—of whom there are relatively few, all things considered—are orphans, cripples and elderly persons who have no families to care for them. A 50-piastre note (worth a little less than 10 cents American) brings joy to their faces, even though it won't cover the price of a soft drink at the nearest sidewalk stand.

This reporter visited a couple of shantytowns on the outskirts of Saigon. An America of another day would have called them Hoovervilles,[1] but there was a big difference. There was no noticeable atmosphere of depression; on the contrary, husbands went off to whatever work they could find, wives took care of the house and the younger children while the older children went to school if possible, all with a general atmosphere of cheerful well-being. There was no moaning and groaning about the situation; the people went about the business of getting through today with what they had, and didn't complain about what they lacked. This reporter never had seen shantytowns before, but there they

[1] A reference to the shack-like towns in which lived many of the poor who were unemployed during the depression years of the 1930s when Herbert Hoover was President of the United States.

were—walls of cardboard and scrap wood, roofs of sheet metal. And they were immaculate. There are many physically superior places in America where one is much less inclined to sit and linger.

The Vietnamese poor have one big advantage over their western cousins —unlike America and some other western countries, where the poor minority often is looked down upon by most of the richer majority, in Saigon so many people could be classed as "poor" (at least by U.S. standards) that nobody seems ashamed to be poor. Most poor parents nourish hopes that their children will do better than they, but they don't mope about their status; they're too busy earning some sort of livelihood to put the next bowl of soup on the table.

Most of the Vietnamese poor have heard about America, and they'll ask a visitor about life in the United States, including the status of the poor. So one tries to explain what things are like in U.S. ghettos, but the reply frequently is a puzzled look.

Why?

Because Americans really don't know what poverty is.

How do you explain leaky plumbing to someone whose only lavatory is the nearest gutter?

How do you explain crumbling plaster to someone whose only roof is the open sky?

What Do you Think? _____

1. The author notes that while most Saigonese live in indescribable poverty it doesn't seem to bother them because there is no stigma attached. Might poverty in some ways be psychological? Explain.

2. Do the poor in America show the same ability to get back up and try again when fate knocks them down?

3. Would you agree with the statement "Americans really don't know what poverty is"? Why or why not?

3. The Extent of Poverty in America*

This selection summarizes some of the major arguments of those who believe that there are too many poor people in America.

Writing in 1963, Leon Keyserling, an economist and former Chairman of the President's Council of Economic Advisers, stated that:

*David A. Durfee.

[T]he number of families living in poverty with incomes under $3,000 . . . was 8.9 million or an estimated 29.2 million people. The number of unattached individuals living in poverty, with incomes under $1,500, was 5 million. The total number of people living in poverty thus came to 34.2 million, or between a fifth and sixth of a nation.

More tragically still, in 1963 the number of families with incomes under $2,000 was 5.1 million, or 16.7 million people. And the number of unattached individuals with incomes under $1,000 was 3.2 million. Thus, almost 20 million people, or substantially more than a tenth of a nation, were at least 33⅓ percent *below* the income levels needed to lift them out of the poverty celler.

And none of the data just cited convey the full meaning of poverty. For the *average* income of all families under $3,000 in 1963 was only $1,778; the *average* for all families "under $2,000" was only $1,220; the *average* for the 1.8 families "under $1,000" was only $630.[1]

Professor Keyserling also described a category he called deprivation. People in this class were ones with incomes that were above the poverty line but at least $1,000 below the amount needed for a "modest but adequate" standard of living. He found about 32 million living in deprivation. Adding this 32 million to the 34.2 million people living below the poverty line he arrived at an estimate of 66 million poor Americans, just about one-third of the population.

Since 1963 the United States has been through a "War on Poverty." Some cases of poverty were ended, the poor became more self-aware, and some services for the poor were established[2] —but no one has claimed that the "war" was really won. There are indeed probably fewer than 66 million poor and deprived in America today. The Bureau of the Census estimated that the country was down to 25.6 million below the poverty line by 1971. This may be considered as the minimum number of poor in the 70's. The maximum number would be about 50 million, arrived at by adding about 24 million in the deprived category to the 25.6 million below the poverty line.

If the 50 million figure is true, it means about one-fourth of the American people are living in poverty. If the 25.6 million figure is true, it still means about one-eighth.

Certainly not every one of the people below the deprivation line, or even the poverty line, is actually poor. There are undoubtedly some who had low income in the census year but high incomes the year before and the year after; there are undoubtedly some college students with very little income who shouldn't be classed as poor; and there are undoubtedly people who receive generous amounts of goods and services instead of money income and are

[1] Leon H. Keyserling, *Progress or Poverty: The U.S. at the Crossroads* (Washington, D.C.: Conference on Economic Progress, 1964).
[2] Roger Wilkins, "The War on Poverty: Ten Years Later," *The New York Times,* June 4, 1974.

therefore not poor. But the opposites would be true, as well. There are undoubtedly some who had high incomes during the census year who haven't had them before or since, and there are undoubtedly individuals with large incomes but overwhelming debts or expenses who are actually poor.

Those whose poverty was ended by the War on Poverty were generally those that were the easiest cases, people who just needed a little boost. Even if the Bureau of the Census is right and the percent of the population living in poverty is only 12.5, that remaining 12.5 percent is made up mostly of the really hard-core cases, the people who need a lot, not just a little help.

But the actual figures are likely to be considerably higher than those of the Bureau because the poor tend to be hard to count, as in the case of the constantly moving migrant workers, and because inflation has forced many new people into the ranks of the poor. By the mid 1970's, for example, Washington columnist Jack Anderson could begin one of his columns by noting:

> Soaring prices are driving the poor, particularly old people with fixed incomes, to eating cheap dog and cat foods. This is the stark finding of a confidential Senate nutrition study.[3]

What Do You Think?

1. The figures indicate that at least one American out of eight lives in poverty. Do your own experiences and observations confirm this, or do you think the figure is too high or too low?

2. Who all should be counted in determining the number of poor in America? Only those living in absolute poverty? All those below the poverty line? All those who are unable to afford a "modest but adequate" standard of living?

3. Do you agree with the idea that those who are still poor after the War on Poverty are probably more difficult cases than those whose poverty was ended during the "War"?

4. Is the United States Really Filled with Poverty?*

Some experts have been very critical of all figures which indicate that there are millions and millions of poor in America. They argue that you cannot determine whether or not a person lives in poverty just by looking at how much money he makes. The following selection, for example, suggests that if the way in which people with low incomes live is examined, it will prove that the number of poor and deprived people in America has been grossly exaggerated.

[3]Jack Anderson, "Washington Merry-Go-Round," *Washington Post,* June 19, 1974.
*By John B. Parrish, Professor of Economics, University of Illinois. Reprinted from *U.S. News & World Report.* Copyright © 1967 U.S. News & World Report, Inc.

When future historians write the history of the 1960's, there will be no more extraordinary episode in their accounts than the rise of America's "new poverty" cult. Intellectuals from every social-science discipline, every religious denomination, every political and social institution have climbed aboard the poverty bandwagon.

This article is concerned with a few fundamental questions: How did the new cult get started? What are its claims? Does the economic evidence support the claims? Are we moving toward a new and better social order or toward social chaos?

After a decade of exploring every nook and cranny of the poverty world, the "new poverty" cult has settled on a few basic doctrines which together form a dogma that apparently must be accepted on faith. These claims may be briefly summarized as follows:

1. The economic process, which in earlier years brought affluence to a major-ity of Americans, recently has slowed up and apparently stopped. As a result, a large minority of Americans are "hopelessly" trapped below the poverty line.

2. The size of this poverty population is "massive," and may be increasing. Minimum estimates place the number at 30 million, maximum at nearly 80 million.

3. Despite its great size, the poverty population is hidden away—"invisible," unknown, unwanted, unaided, helpless.

4. The hard core of the "other America" is the Negro. Because of racial discrimination, he has been unable to participate in economic progress. He is frustrated, embittered, forced to live outside the affluent society of the majority.

5. The "new poverty" can only be eradicated by massive, federal social-action programs involving income maintenance, self-help, education and training, in a milieu of racial integration, the latter voluntary if possible, compulsory if necessary.

Does the evidence on diffusion of economic well-being support the "new poverty" cult? Has diffusion mysteriously slowed to a halt leaving millions "hopelessly trapped"? Are 30 to 80 million suffering acute deprivation in today's America? The plain truth is there is no basis in fact for the "new poverty" thesis. The high priests of the poverty religion have been exchanging each other's misinformation. Let's look briefly at some illustrative evidence.

Diet. The diet of U.S. families has continued to improve steadily over time until today at least 95 percent, perhaps 96 percent or 97 percent of all families have an adequate minimum daily intake of nutrients.

Automatic cooking equipment. Are 20 percent, perhaps 40 percent, of U.S. families without decent equipment with which to prepare this food in-take? No. As a matter of fact, 99 percent of all U.S. households have automatic cooking equipment, including most of those families living in rural and urban "ghettos." The diffusion has been consistent and persistent over the last six decades.

Refrigeration. Could it be that millions of American families are experiencing dull and dreary meals because they have no way to preserve foods and beverages against spoilage? No. About 99 percent of all U.S. families have purchased electric or gas refrigerators. It is reasonable to assume they know how to operate them, even in the "ghettos."

Communication. Are millions of America's poor shut off from all contact with the rest of their affluent countrymen—Alone, frustrated, in that "other world" of poverty isolation? At last count, the diffusion of TV sets had reached 92 percent of all U.S. households, providing instant access to entertainment, news, sports, cultural enrichment. Since a small percent of middle and upper income families who can afford TV have chosen not to buy, the percent of families having TV who want it must be around 96 or 97 percent—a diffusion achieved in just 15 years.

Medical aid. Have the "new helpless poor" found the doors to modern medical service "slammed shut," forcing them to rely on quack remedies, superstition, midwives, or to die alone and unattended?

In 1910 only one in every 10 American families had access to hospitals for childbirth. The diffusion since then has been spectacular and persistent for all groups, including nonwhites. By 1960, over 97 percent of all American women had their babies born in hospitals. Today it is somewhere between 98 percent and 99 percent.

The luxury of telephone service. Telephone service is ordinarily not a rock-bottom consumer necessity. It is useful and convenient but not an absolute requirement, as was demonstrated during the Great Depression of the 1930's when the percent of families with telephones declined.

Yet today nearly 90 percent of all U.S. households have telephones. Since there are still a few pockets of unavailability, it is reasonable to conclude that close to 95 percent of all U.S. households in availability areas who would like this luxury actually enjoy it.

"Three Poverty Fallacies"

The foregoing illustrative evidence raises an interesting question: *How can the "massive" group of America's "hopeless poor" buy so much with so little?* Perhaps this basis question can be put another way: How could the poverty intellectuals be so wrong? The answer is actually very simple. The intellectuals have chosen to be wrong. Most members of the "new poverty" cult are quite well-trained in statistics. Some are acknowledged experts. They know better. But, for the sake of the "new poverty" religion, they have chosen to accept three poverty fallacies.

The "new poverty" cult has built much of its case on family-income statistics. Some technical matters aside, there is nothing wrong with these statistics, per se. But there is something wrong, very much wrong, with their use. It is impossible for anyone adequately to interpret them in terms of average family economic well-being.

Poverty fallacy No. 1 got its big push from the 1964 report on "The Problem of Poverty in America" by the Council of Economic Advisers. CEA determined that households with less than $3,000 annual income were in poverty. Using this income yardstick, it was determined that 20 percent of U.S. households containing 30 million persons were in the poverty class.

This report provided a wonderful takeoff point for poverty statisticians. With 30 million to build on, it was not difficult to find millions of additional families who should be added to the poverty population. The poverty numbers game became quite exciting. Who could count the most? Honors so far have gone to those claiming nearly 80 million. A majority of cult members have settled for a more modest 40 to 50 million.

The truth about poverty-income statistics is this: Under no reasonable assumptions does any income below $3,000 indicate poverty status. It may or may not, and to say otherwise is not only erroneous but absurd.

Let's take as an example a young married couple, the Smiths. They are attending college. They constitute a statistical household. Their annual income is $1,500 a year. They are not being "hopelessly" shut out from the good things of life. They are, along with other American youth, enjoying a rate of access to higher education greater than the youth of any country, any time, any place. They enjoy electric lighting, refrigeration, adequate if not fancy food, and a second-hand automobile or motorcycle. They would like a new Cadillac, but will manage without one. They aren't "poor" and need no crocodile tears shed in their behalf.

At the other end of the life cycle are the Joneses. Mr. Jones has been a machinist all his life. He and Mrs. Jones had always wanted to visit the country's great national parks after the children had grown up and left. So he has opted to retire at age 60. The retirement income will come to only $2,000 a year. Are they poor? The poverty cult says, "Yes," these people are suffering from deprivation. They have been "hopelessly" cast aside. Yet the truth is they have a small home paid for, a modest automobile paid for. They enjoy refrigeration, automatic cooking equipment, inside plumbing, TV, enough clothes to last for years—the accumulation of a lifetime. And now they propose to enjoy more leisure, in more comfort, for more years than similar working-class families of any country, any time. The Joneses think the Council of Economic Advisers is statistically wacky.

And take the Browns. They are in the middle years. Both Mr. and Mrs. Brown work. Their three children are in school. They have a modest new home, partially paid for, some savings, some insurance, good clothes—yes, and a paid-for refrigerator and TV set. They have a new car and six installments still outstanding. Mr. Brown becomes ill. Mrs. Brown quits work to take care of him. Their income drops to below $3,000 for the year. Are they in trouble? Yes. Are they in desperate consumer poverty? Are they "hopelessly trapped"? By no means. After a tough year they will resume as members of the affluent society even by CEA's definition.

Economic Well-Being: "Cumulative"

These illustrations could be multiplied many times. Cross-section household-income statistics are a very inappropriate yardstick with which   **49**

to measure economic well-being, which is a longitudinal and cumulative process. . . .

There is a second big fallacy in the "new poverty" claims, and in some respects an inexcusable one. The poverty cult measures the economic well-being of families at all income levels by determining what they can buy with their income at current retail prices. In fact, the poverty cult makes much out of the fact that because of the greed of retail merchants and the gullibility and lack of buying savvy on the part of many poor buyers, the "new poor" actually pay more for the same goods than the affluent classes. This is hogwash.

The truth is, America's low-income classes have access to a low-price consumer-goods market in which prices are a fraction of published retail prices, and in which the purchasing power of "poor" dollars is multiplied many times. This discount market yields levels of consumption far above that indicated by retail prices.

As the poor could explain to CEA and the poverty intellectuals, this market is America's enormously big resale market—the world's largest. Every year, from 25 to 65 percent of many consumer durable-goods purchases involve second- or third-hand goods moving in established trade or in informal person-to-person channels. . . .

Growth of No-Cost Goods, Services

If ignoring the durable-goods resale market is inexcusable, the failure of

the poverty cult to take account of the rapid growth in low-cost or no-cost goods and services in America is well-nigh incredible. It is incredible because much of it has been brought about by the very federal agencies whose economists have been among the high priests of the poverty cult. This failure constitutes poverty fallacy No. 3.

To illustrate: Nearly 90 percent of all Negro births today are in hospitals. Yet the U.S. House Committee on Education and Labor in 1964 said half the Negroes in America were suffering from acute poverty, measured by income statistics. How can so many poor afford so much medical service? For two reasons: First, as already noted, the income data are faulty. But more to the point here, almost every urban community has free or very low-cost medical services for low-income families. In fact, surveys show that in some communities the lowest-income families have more medical checkups, vaccinations, chest X-rays, eye examinations than some higher income groups.

The number of low-cost food programs has been growing rapidly. For example, the national school-lunch program provided low-cost noon meals for nearly 20 million children in 1967. The food-stamp plan provided low-cost food for 1 million persons in 1966, and was scheduled to rise to 2 million in 1967. The low-cost milk plan, along with school lunch, accounted for 5 percent of total U.S. nonfarm fluid-milk consumption in 1966, and would have expanded even more in 1967 had not cutbacks been ordered because of Vietnam.

The total number of low-income persons reached by various food-subsidy programs came to nearly 30 million in 1966, or precisely the number of persons classified as poor in 1964 by the Council of Economic Advisers. Since many of the CEA's 30 million didn't belong in the poverty classification in the first place, some questions may well be raised as to who and how many poor have been "forgotten."

What Do You Think?

1. Is possession of or lack of consumer durable goods such as refrigerators, washing machines, and TV sets a better standard for determining poverty or affluence than family income? Why or why not?

2. A study made in 1968 indicated that 10 million Americans suffered from hunger and malnutrition. How do these figures compare with those given by the author of this reading? How can you explain the differences in the way in which they are stated?

3. The author states that many who have claimed much higher numbers of poor than he believes exist "know better" than some of the claims they make and that they are guilty of inexcusable fallacies. Would anyone want to find more poverty than actually existed? Explain. Would anyone want to find less? Explain.

4. Is it possible that people who pay less for second-hand items may end up spending more in the long run because these items break down or wear out so quickly?

5. A Single Ice Cream Cone Each Morning*

Inflation has made it even harder to determine just how many really poor people there are in America. As prices of necessities have gone up, income that would have been adequate a few weeks before has suddenly become completely inadequate. James T. Wooten looked into the effects of inflation on the poor in February 1975.

When Mrs. Elsie DeFratus could no longer afford the cost of living, she died.

She was nearly 80 years old, and she had survived somehow for a long, long time on her meager widow's pension, frugally measuring it against the rising prices, scrimping and scraping and skipping meals, making do with less and less each day until finally, on a recent morning at an ancient hotel in this city, she crumpled quietly to the floor of her dark and tiny apartment.

She weighed 76 pounds. An autopsy found no trace of food in her shrunken stomach.

"Malnutrition," the coroner concluded.

"Surrender," sighed an elderly friend. "She stopped believing tomorrow would be better."

Both may have been right, but in any case the small, emaciated woman had become the ultimate victim of inflation. Her extremity had gone as far as it could go.

For millions of other Americans, inflation's effect has been not as extreme, but it is hurting deeply nonetheless.

From one end of the country to the other, in rural hollows and small-town slums, in prairie reservations and mountain enclaves and city ghettos, it attacks the poor, the elderly, those on fixed incomes. Sometimes, it leaves them, like Mrs. DeFratus, both hungry and hopeless.

One of the poor, Robert Davis, sat at his kitchen table in the tiny dinette of his housing-project apartment in Little Rock recently, talking with his wife and some visitors about the way he believes other people see him.

"I don't think they think much of me," he said, staring at his mud-caked, high-top shoes. "I mean, they don't think I've amounted to much as a man. Used to be, I didn't much care what they thought, but nowadays—well, I don't know. Maybe they're right."

Mr. Davis is a 40-year-old black man who works more than 40 hours almost every week on a construction crew and earns slightly more than $2 an hour. Occasionally he takes odd jobs on Saturdays to supplement his weekly earnings.

"It wasn't hardly ever enough," he said. "Not with nine kids at home. But there was a time there not too far back when we were sort of looking up. Now, I don't see nothing but down."

Soup and Crackers

As he talked, his wife quietly prepared dinner for the family, a meal consisting of chicken soup, some crackers, milk for the younger children and coffee for the older ones. She is 38 years old.

She cannot remember a single moment in all of her life, she said, when she was not lacking something she really needed.

Her husband said: "I know people look at us and laugh and say how come we got so many kids, and I say it's because we always wanted a bunch of them and because I never did know we was going to be poor."

Mrs. Davis laughed—a slight chuckle barely heard above the sounds of her puttering at the stove.

Mr. Davis went on: "I always thought that the way I could work—I'm a right strong man—that we'd make it some way. Now, tell the truth, I don't think we can."

In the last few months, their utility bills have gone from $8 to $21 each month, the result of a rate increase by the local power company. The cost of their groceries has risen from about $60 a week to more than $100, even when Mrs. Davis buys less than she believes they need.

A few weeks ago, with several auto loan installments long overdue, they chose to pay for their food and their water and their lights and their shelter, and the finance company repossessed their second-hand car.

They pay $33 each month for their cramped, dark quarters, and, should Mrs. Davis take a job, the rent would increase proportionately and make the added income almost inconsequential.

"You know them beans I use to buy, Robert?" she said softly. "You know, those dried beans—Lord, I guess I've cooked a ton of them—and they used to be four pounds for 59 cents. You know how much they are now, Robert?"

Mr. Davis shook his head.

"Just guess, Robert," she said.

He declined silently.

"Well, they're $2 for four pounds, that's what they are, and we just can't buy them any more," she said.

Still her husband said nothing.

"You know what, Robert?" Mrs. Davis said, turning away from the stove for a moment. "I think you're right."

"What's that?" he asked.

"I don't think we're going to make it either."

* * * * *

In New York, Detroit, Miami and Chicago, there have been arrests of elderly citizens—some of them extremely feeble—for stealing groceries in order to eat.

"But Elsie never would have done that," said Steven Haddock, manager of the hotel where Mrs. DeFratus lived here on the Sunshine Coast of Florida. "She just wouldn't have stolen anything."

Instead, she chose to attempt to manage on her Social Security checks of less than $100 a month, and with the cost of her room, $15 a week, and her transportation to and from the Post Office to pick up her check, her food allowance was down to less than 65 cents a day.

Frequently, when her funds were nearly depleted toward the end of the month, she would settle for a single ice cream cone each morning, and somehow it had always been enough.

But on Oct. 3, after carefully arranging her clothes on her bed, she collapsed to the floor and died. Her Social Security check arrived the same day.

What Do You Think? _____

1. Why is inflation a more serious problem for people like Mrs. DeFratus and the Davis family than for most Americans?
2. If Mr. Davis' wages do not go up as fast as prices, why doesn't he quit and find a job that pays more?
3. Which is more serious, the decline in the amount of food they can buy or the way in which inflation seems to wipe out all hope for the future?

ACTIVITIES FOR INVOLVEMENT

1. Reread the selections in Chapter 3, all of which describe specific situations. As you read note all evidence of the amount of income and of whether or not the people enjoy the goods and services described by Parrish. Do the readings support or dispute the idea that amount of income is a good measure of poverty or affluence?

2. In 1963 Keyserling reported that of 34 million Americans with income under the poverty level:

   - 52 percent reflect deficient education;
   - 44 percent live in the South;
   - 40 percent reflect excessive unemployment;
   - 29 percent reflect female family heads;
   - 27 percent reflect aged family heads;
   - 25 percent are nonwhite;
   - 15 percent live on farms.

   Arrange these categories in the order of the "hopelessness" of the condition. Be prepared to defend your arrangement. Compare your listing with those of your classmates. What differences do you notice? Similarities? How would you explain these differences and similarities?

3. Write a description similar in style to those of the Smiths, Joneses, and Browns in the second reading in this chapter. Try to describe families and individuals as close to the poverty line as possible, with some just above it and some just below. Share your descriptions with the rest of the class. Do all members of the class agree as to which cases are really poverty cases? Hold a class discussion in which you try to establish standards that can be used to determine whether or not a person lives in poverty.

4. In 1973 and 1974 the world oil crisis brought about a rise in unemployment, while inflation continued to lower buying power. Do some research (consult the *Reader's Guide*) and make a report on how families handled their reduced income or changed their life styles. Compare these studies and discuss in class which, if any, of these people should be considered poor. Would they consider themselves poor?

5
WHAT
CAUSES
POVERTY?

In earlier societies it was easy to explain the presence of poverty. There just wasn't enough to go around and so some people had to do without. It is not so easy to explain in an affluent society where there is more than enough to go around.

How can poverty in America today be explained then? There are several possible ways. There are those who argue that it exists because there are some people in the society who are too lazy or too lacking in character to take care of themselves. There are others who argue that it is the result of historical or economic forces beyond the power of man to control. Others see the root of poverty in discrimination and say that poverty exists because the well-to-do want it to exist. Some see it as the result of unwise actions that the government has taken. Finally, there are those who see it as different in every case and argue that we must look at the poor as individuals and find the unique set of causes for their poverty.

Which are the correct explanations? Or is it possible that all are partly correct? What does cause poverty?

1. "Why Should They Work When They Can Get Welfare?"*

There are many people who see lack of ambition or weakness of character on the part of the poor themselves as the primary causes of poverty. There were several students who felt this way in the social studies class in which the following exchange took place.

The class was in the middle of a discussion of current news. Tony had just reported hearing an item on a local radio station. Officials were predicting a sharp rise in county taxes.

Sally: "That makes three, then, the income tax, the state tax, and this; all going up."

*David A. Durfee. A composite of two discussions held in a social studies class in Sleepy Hollow High School, North Tarrytown, N.Y.

Teacher: "Does the idea bother you?"

Sally: "Well, sure. The way things are going, we're all going to be working for the government pretty soon. Taxes are too high already. They ought to lower them rather than raise them. I mean, we can't afford taxes like these."

Al: (Interrupting) "You don't pay 'em."

Sally: "You know what I mean. My parents do and that affects me. I mean, my parents pay them and that's less that they can spend for college and other things for me."

Teacher: "Do many of you really have to do without things you need because of taxes?"

(Silence and some looking around)

Tony: "It's not so much that. It's that the government wastes most of the money."

Teacher: "Really?"

Tony: "Maybe not 'most,' but a lot."

Frank: "You know that whenever the government does something it costs more. Every politician has to get something out of it."

Mary Louise: "Never say, 'Every.' "

Frank: "O.K., O.K."

Art: "Anyway, the thing that really takes a lot of money and makes the taxes go up is the welfare. We wouldn't need any of these tax increases, except maybe the national one, if they'd make everybody on welfare go to work."

Teacher: "Are there many people on welfare who are able to work who aren't?"

Several students: "Yes!"

Teacher: "How do you know?"

Frank: "My father has been trying to hire a man to clean up at his shop. He's gone down to the state employment office lots of times. He's talked to some of the welfare men there and had a couple who came up here. They don't want to work. They make up some sort of excuses when they learn what kind of work it is. Sure, maybe if you offered them a nice desk job at $20,000 a year and no real work they'd be glad to take it. But when they learn that he wants them to clean up they say they've got bad backs or can't get transportation or don't want to be too far from home. One guy drove up in a big Buick— my father saw him—but when he learned he'd have to sweep the floors he said he didn't have any way to get to the job. My father asked him, 'What about that Buick?' and he said, 'Oh, I just borrowed it.' He probably owns it and is paying for it with his welfare money."

Mary Louse: "We've had the same trouble trying to get a cleaning lady. You ask them to do some ironing because there isn't enough cleaning to take the whole day and they say, 'Oh, I'm not supposed to do that.' Then, if my mother insists, she does a careless job and then the next week calls up and says she's sick. You try to make them work and they quit. Why should they work when they can get welfare?"

Liz: "I'm sure that there are some people on welfare who should be working, but just because you have come across one or two doesn't mean that they are all like that or that there are so many they make our taxes high."

Sally: "We do have a good cleaning lady who's one of them, but she says that everybody else where she lives is just living off welfare."

Liz: "Just how many is 'everybody'? You see two or three and you're angry because you work hard and they don't and you say 'everybody.' I'd like to know how many she means."

Sally: "Lots."

Tony: "There are plenty of jobs around. There's one station that broadcasts lists of jobs every week and you hear the same job week after week. You can say you've got to take care of poor people and, sure, you've got to if they're crippled or something. But most people if they're poor it's just because they're too lazy to work."

Liz: "Maybe they don't have enough education to get the jobs."

Tony: "What education do you need to clean up a shop or be a cleaning lady or a dishwasher? Anyway, if they don't have a good education it's their own fault. There are free schools for all, you know."

Frank: "Some people are on welfare and their parents were on welfare and their kids will be on welfare. It doesn't make sense, this whole system. Anybody can get on welfare and obviously nobody will work if he can get money without working."

Teacher: "Do you all agree with that?"

Voice from rear: "With what?"

Teacher: "That anybody can get on welfare and that no one will work if he can get income without doing any work."

Several: "Yes."

Teacher: "Then I'm going to ask you to raise your hands to show me something. Maybe I'm missing out on a good thing. I'm going to ask first to see the hands of those of you who are planning to take advantage of this system and go on welfare and—just a second—then to see the hands of those who are planning to work for a living or marry a man who will work for a living. Now, how many of you plan to go on welfare?"

(A few, "But that isn't . . ." but no hands.)

"How many plan to work?"

(Most hands up, but not all.)

"But you said anybody can go on welfare and that everybody would want to get the money without working for it. Are you different from everybody? Why are you planning to work? And what about you, Sue, you didn't choose either. Does welfare tempt you?"

Rick: "No, she's planning to marry a rich guy."

Teacher: "We'd better not get off on that. Why didn't the rest of you choose welfare?"

Frank: "Because we're not lazy the way they are and we're working hard enough in school to get jobs that pay a lot more than welfare."

Teacher: "I didn't realize that you were so ambitious and like to work so much. Let me give you a couple of extra reading assign. . . ."

Rick: "We wouldn't want you to go to any trouble."

Teacher: "Back to the question, then. You are saying that there are enough jobs so that no one needs to be poor but that there are some people **59** who are not hard working the way we are and are too lazy to take jobs and that it is these people who are on welfare?"

Liz: "Not just too lazy. We said that there were some who didn't have a good enough education."

Teacher: "I'm not sure that everyone agreed with that, Liz. Would you accept this? There are enough jobs and that there are opportunities for education for those who need it to take the jobs so no one needs to be poor, but some people are too lazy and so they're poor and on welfare."

Frank: "Yes."

Liz: "I don't. ...."

Sally: "Pretty much, yes. I mean, there are some people who are crippled or something and aren't lazy."

Teacher: "I think we all accept that."

Sally: "There ought to be a law saying that those who can work should or no welfare. I mean, if they refuse to work let them do without. They'll learn."

Teacher: "Isn't there such a law?"

Sally: "I don't know, but if there is they don't enforce it."

Teacher: "I was doing some work the other day *(Laughter)* and came across some figures. They went like this." *(Writes on board.)*

- 7.3 million people on welfare
- 2.1 million are 65 or over
- .7 million are blind or severely handicapped
- 3.5 million are children whose parents can't support them
- .75 million are mothers of these children
- .1 million are fathers of these children who are incapacitated
- .05 million are people who could be self-supporting.

"Do these support the idea that the poor are poor just because they are lazy?"

Tony: "I bet a lot of those men who claim to be disabled are faking it. They could work if they wanted to and they would if it weren't for welfare."

Frank: "The important thing in those figures is the mothers and children. If those women go and have children when there's no husband around to take care of them that's their own fault. Why should we have to take care of them and their children just because they behave that way?"

Liz: "Would you make the children suffer just because the mothers aren't married?"

Frank: "There could be homes or something to take care of the kids and we could make the mothers work and pay the homes for taking care of them."

Tony: "Maybe we should add something to what you said before. Poor are poor because their morals are bad."

Liz: "Can we really judge whose morals are bad? Maybe it's their education."

60   *Sally:* "Well certainly. ...' *(Bell.)*

1. This reading is entitled: "Why Should They Work When They Can Get Welfare?" How would you answer this question? Explain your reasoning.
2. If there are some people who won't work because they can get welfare benefits equal to or greater than the amount they could earn, should this be ended by lowering welfare benefits or by raising wages? Explain.
3. Was Frank correct in assuming that the man really owned the Buick? What is the basis for your opinion?
4. Tony states: "Anyway, if they (the poor) don't have a good education it's their own fault. There are free schools for all, you know." How would you respond to this?
5. To what extent can the poor be directly blamed for the poverty in which they live?

2. Promises Unfulfilled*

Poverty in some sections of the country can be explained in terms of the history and economic development of those areas. Certainly the poverty found on the Indian reservation described in Chapter 3 cannot be understood without remembering the things that were done to the Indian in earlier days. In the same way, as the following selection shows, what happened in Appalachia in the past affects that region today.

The poor of Appalachia are, in a very real sense, victims of history. This region, stretching from Georgia and Alabama in the south to Pennsylvania in the north and including large sections of West Virginia, Virginia, Kentucky, Tennessee, and North Carolina, has offered much but given little to its residents.

Appalachia has promised people a better way of life several times. These promises have lured people into the area and have kept them there.

The first promises were land, game, and freedom. Most of the early settlers were poorer people who had come to America from England, Scotland, and Ireland. Most had come voluntarily, but a few had been brought by force. As more and more of the tidewater lands were taken over by the large plantations, these poorer people moved to the west. There were game animals in the forests; there was land available in the valleys and coves (small recesses or areas between higher ground, very narrow where they start on the sides of the hills but becoming wider as they move down toward the broader valleys

* By David A. Durfee. See Harry Caudill, *Night Comes to the Cumberlands: A Biography of a Depressed Area* (Boston, Mass.: Little, Brown & Co. 1963), and Jack Weller, *Yesterday's People —Life in Contemporary Appalachia* (Louisville, Ky.: University of Kentucky Press, 1965).

below); there was a chance to be independent. They settled in the valleys and moved up into the coves. As population increased they were forced farther up the coves until they reached areas where farming was nearly impossible. To meet the need for more land, they began to farm the hillsides. This led to erosion and new difficulties. It was possible to live on the game and on the produce of poor farms, but it was not possible to live well. Of the three promises, land, game, and freedom, only the last was really fulfilled. The mountaineer was independent and he has cherished his independence and individualism ever since.

The second great promise of prosperity came from the forests. When the settlers had arrived, the mountains had been covered with magnificent trees, especially hardwoods such as oak and poplar. In the late nineteenth century speculators moved into the area offering what seemed fantastic sums to the mountaineers for the right to cut down and remove the trees from their land. In reality, the sums were nowhere near the true value of the timber. The mountaineer retained ownership of the land but the trees were the property of the speculator or the corporation to which he sold them. There was a wave of prosperity. In addition to the money he received for selling the timber rights, the mountaineer could earn wages performing dangerous logging operations. When the wave of prosperity ended, the mountains were barer and more eroded than before and the mountaineers were worse off than they had been before.

The last and greatest promise of prosperity was coal. The purchase of mineral rights reached its peak around the turn of the century. Mountaineers sold the rights for from $.50 to $5.00 an acre. A great industry and great fortunes were built on minerals that had once been the property of the mountaineers.

Coal mining brought destruction to much of the beauty of the region. Great mountains of discarded coal and slate grew. These frequently caught fire and remained burning slowly for years. Coal dust and smoke filled the air.

If ownership and beauty were gone, there were at least great employment opportunities. Prosperity was greatest during the period from World War I until the Depression. The population grew and it appeared that there would always be jobs for all. This was not to be, however. As the use of oil and gas and then atomic energy for fuel grew, the demand for coal declined. In order to compete with the producers of these other fuels, the coal companies replaced workers with machinery. Employment went way down and has stayed down ever since.

There are poor people in Appalachia today. People lured there by riches that no longer exist. People who no longer have either the treasures that the area had or the money they got for the sale of those treasures. Many of the younger people have moved out. The older folks have nothing to do but stay and get along somehow.

What Do You Think?

1. Is there any way in which the people of these mountains could have developed the riches themselves instead of selling them to outsiders? Where would they have gotten the capital needed to develop them?

2. Which do you think is the most important reason for the presence of poverty in Appalachia today, the kind of people who moved there in the first place, the out-of-the-way location of Appalachia, or the way in which the timber and coal resources were exploited? Explain your reasoning.

3. There are not enough jobs in Appalachia today. Would it be better to try to move new industries into the area or move the people who live there out? Explain.

3. Progress is the Enemy*

Coal miners aren't the only people suffering unemployment because of the development of new machines. In a modern industrial state the pace of technological change is very rapid. Every day in both cities and rural areas men who have been trained to do a job are replaced by machines that can do the same job more rapidly and more economically. The situation is most tragic in the cases of those who are too old to learn a new skill or those who are capable only of unskilled labor in a land where it is no longer needed.

Cleosa Henley, whose hunger was described in Chapter 3, and others like him face this tragedy in the Black Belt.

* From "Lord, I'm Hungry." Copyright © Newsweek, Inc., July 24, 1967, reprinted by permission.

Cleosa Henley and thousands of Negroes like him are the DP's [Displaced Persons] of a quiet revolution in the old cotton south. Once they were a fixed part of the landscape of the Black Belt, the fertile black crescent that runs thickest through Georgia, Alabama and Mississippi. But new cash crops (soybeans, wheat, timber, cattle) and a new cotton technology (mechanical pickers, chemical weed-killers) have made the old hoe hand expendable. The $1-an-hour minimum wage that went into effect for farm workers this year made him uneconomical. And the civil rights revolt, once it put the ballot in his hands, made him downright frightening to whites in areas with black majorities. Poor to begin with, the cottonfield Negro today is virtually obsolete—and poorer and hungrier than ever.

In this world, progress is often the enemy, and even the best intended government efforts to help sometimes become cruel jokes. Thus, the $1 minimum wage only spurred the Alabama Black Belt's interest in new crops. Greene County laid in its first 600 acres of soybeans in 1965, planted 17,000 acres [in 1967]—more than double the cotton acreage. "When we got rid of our niggers," says one planter, who has bulldozed most of his 200 tenant shacks, "we found out what money was." The wage law similarly sped up the delta's thrust into the technology of chemicals and machines. The tractor drivers stayed on, though—with The Man keeping the books—$1 an hour tends to melt down to the same take home pay they got under the old rate of $6 a day. The real victims are the tenant wives and children and the "day haul" laborers who used to chop weeds in the spring and hand-pick cotton in the fall for $3 a day. The number of Negro pickers in the delta shrank, by one estimate, from 60,000 in 1959 to 2,000 [in 1966]—most of them working the edges of the fields where the machines miss a bit.

"Eliminatin' "

But more than blind economic chance is at work. "Them white folks got a lot more interested in machinery after the civil rights bill was passed," one Black Belt Negro muses—and it is certainly true that the rights revolt has eroded Dixie's ancient paternalism. In the thickly wooded north end of Greene County, Alabama, "Miss Mary" Hixon, an ancient, feisty widow, still lives in her family's colonnaded ante-bellum mansion—and her thinned-out colony of tenants still occupies the old slave quarters out back. But Miss Mary has sold off much of her holdings to out-of-state buyers. "I wept bitterly when I sold the land," she says, "and all my nigras wept. But I couldn't keep 'em—they wouldn't work a lick. Ever since they got that civil rights bill they all figure the gov'ment will take care of them. I'll tell you one thing—if I was head of the Ku Klux, there'd be some eliminatin'."

"We thought if we lost our niggers, the world would come to an end," says another of the county's planters, Dave Johnston. But now he's recruiting white families in Missouri to work his 8,000 acres, much of it planted with soybeans, and he says: "The niggers is got to go. . . . It's like the deer. We got a lotta trouble with the deer eatin' our soybeans. We just wanta thin 'em out to where we can live with 'em."

64

What Do You Think?

1. Did the adoption of the civil rights voting act cause white owners to become more interested in machinery, or was it a coincidence that new crops like soybeans came in at the same time? What clues can you find in the reading?
2. Are minimum wage laws for farm workers likely to do such workers more harm or good in the long run?
3. What future would you predict for the "white families from Missouri" that were being recruited to work on the Johnston farm? Explain.

4. No Access to "Access"*

Poverty can be explained in terms of the failings of the poor themselves. It can also be explained in terms of efforts of the well-to-do to protect their position by discriminating against the poor and especially against the minority poor, as the following illustrates.

Many well meaning but misunderstanding whites look deep into the Negro ghettos of our larger cities, shudder at the sight and then say, "Why do they continue living there? Why don't they do like the Irish, the Italians, the Germans, and the Polish? Why don't they move into the mainstream, pull themselves up by their bootstraps, become an integral part of American society?"

These people are laboring under the same misapprehension that has kept most whites from a true understanding of the Negro's position in American history for years—the belief that Negroes have not, as other immigrants, taken advantage of the great rewards supposedly offered by American society to the able, the ambitious and the industrious.

Land of Promise

It is true that the United States, the last great "frontier" country, has been a land of promise to immigrants from nearly every nation in the world. Big, young, and rich in resources, the area which now comprises the United States can look back only 360 years to the establishment of the first English colony in Jamestown, Va., and can count only 191 years as an independent nation. In that short period of time as nations go, the U.S. has been first one of the world's leading agrarian nations and is now one of the most powerful in all history technologically. Science and technology have advanced so rapidly in this century that many persons born before the first successful flight of an

* An *Ebony* editorial by Herbert Nipson. Copyright © 1967, Johnson Publishing Co., Inc. Used by permission.

airplane (the Wright Brothers, 1903) will still be alive to see television films of the first successful landing of a man on the moon.

Considering the tremendous progress of the United States as a whole, it is little wonder that one not familiar with the total history of the country could well ask, "Where has the Negro failed?"

In From the Beginning

To the uninitiated, the plight of the American Negro seems particularly confusing when one considers that the Negro has been a part of this country almost from the beginning. From 1619 until the present, the Negro has been a part of the population of what is now the U.S. From his humble slave beginning, he has grown in number, spread throughout the fifty states and has become a vast influence throughout the nation even though his affluence has lagged behind that of other "immigrants."

The United States is a nation of immigrants or descendants of immigrants. Of all the races and nations which people this country, only the misnamed "American Indian" (called Indian only because the early explorers thought that they had reached India instead of two vast, new continents—North and South America) is indigenous. Following—with two exceptions—the chronology of the waves of immigrants that peopled the U.S., a pecking order of prestige has grown up in this country. At the top is the white, Anglo-Saxon Protestant, descendant of the early colonists, the Daughters of the American Revolution type who too frequently feels that the nation would be much better off if everyone else had stayed home. Other Western Europeans (the Dutch, the German, the Scotch-Irish, French, Scandinavian, and Irish) follow in descending order. Then came the Mediterranean—particularly the Italian—followed by the Jewish, Slavic, Mexican and Latin American, Filipino, Middle Eastern, Oriental, and Puerto Rican.

The exceptions to the chronology are the American Indian, who was here to greet the explorers and colonists when they first arrived, and the Negro who was brought over in chains at about the same time the colonists debarked from their tiny ships. By chronology, they should rank at the top of the pecking order along with the Anglo-Saxon. Instead, they are at the bottom and it is a tossup as to which is in the absolute basement.

No Access to "Access"

The brilliant editor, educator, and author Max Lerner, himself an immigrant who came to the U.S. as a child with his parents from Minsk, Russia, in 1907, was once asked to summarize in a single word the keystone of American development. He answered: "Access. By this I mean access to economic opportunity, access to social mobility, access to geographic movement, access to political participation. Most important of all, perhaps, would be access to educational opportunity."

Dr. Lerner's succinct summing up of the reason America and Americans could advance so readily need only be negatized to give the answers to the questions asked by the well-meaning whites in the first paragraph of this editorial. The American Negro is in the position he is in today because access to practically everything Lerner has mentioned has been denied him while it has remained open to almost every other immigrant who has come to these shores. For his first 244 years in the U.S. the Negro not only had no access to economic opportunity but lived primarily as a slave in a slave economy that made him an economic product to be bought and sold by slave owners. After the Emancipation Proclamation, the Negro found himself free in name only. Trained to work in a slave economy, he found himself the last hired and first fired for more than a century. Performing the hard hand labor, the domestic work, the jobs that no one else wanted, he was lucky to keep food in his children's mouths and a roof over his head. He had no access to the free land available for settlement in the West; he had no access to the gold rushes, the timberland steals, the establishment of new businesses, the free grazing land, the oil explorations, etc. which brought riches to many whites.

No Social Mobility

Dr. Lerner's social mobility was and, with rare exceptions, still is a myth so far as the American Negro is concerned. Even so august a person as the UN's Ralph Bunche found, when he tried to join a tennis club in New York, that a Negro cannot escape his race. Under American society as it is structured today, the Negro has developed a society within a society. A Negro can rise from the slums to middle class, even to wealth within the Negro society and yet have no more status than the slum dweller when the American society as a whole is taken into consideration.

That the Negro has had no true access to full political participation can be proved by the fact that so few Negroes hold statewide offices and by the fact that federal registrars must be sent to many parts of the South just to assure a Negro his right to cast a vote.

Access to educational opportunity is still not something a Negro can take for granted. The children of Grenada, Miss., found themselves brutally beaten by white adults merely because they were attempting to exercise their legal rights to attend an integrated elementary school. Until recent years, many colleges and universities in the North discouraged Negro attendance by not granting Negroes room in dormitories and dining halls. And even today, the Negro ghetto elementary and secondary schools of Northern cities are grossly inferior.

The Right to Travel

The one access mentioned by Dr. Lerner that has been open to Negroes is the access to geographic movement. He has really taken advantage of this access. The Negro left the South literally by the millions, traveling north and west. He spread himself throughout the urban centers of the entire country. **67**

The only trouble was, once he got where he was going he found the other accesses closed to him.

So the next time misunderstanding whites ask, "Why don't they move into the mainstream?" tell them. Tell them to help us open the doors.

What Do You Think? _____

1. Is there a relationship between discrimination and poverty? Is it as direct as this article indicates? Explain your answer.

2. Is there really a "pecking order" in America based on the sequence in which different national groups arrived?

3. Mr. Nipson speaks rather sarcastically of a "Daughters of the American Revolution type." What does he mean by this? How might a member of the D.A.R. respond to this? Explain.

4. If you were to list all of the people you actually know in the order of their social position (where they stand in the "pecking order"), what racial group would you place highest? Lowest?

---

5. Misplaced Emphases in Wars on Poverty*

The first two readings in this chapter presented views placing the blame for poverty on bigotry or laziness. Some experts, however, feel that mistakes made by people with good intentions are at least as important as deliberate actions taken by middle-class whites or lazy welfare recipients.

Simon Rottenberg, Professor of Economics at Duke University, has listed some of the government programs which he believes have helped to produce poverty rather than to lessen it. Portions of his list follow.

An examination of various facets of public policy in the United States will show that some fraction of poverty which we encounter among the people is, in fact, produced by government. Those who promote these policies do not, of course, intend nor desire that they shall have these effects; indeed, some of them are thought to promote progress and ameliorate poverty. Their enactment and execution is a tribute to the power in the world of the naïve cliché. Only some of these poverty-producing policies will be discussed.

1. The Fair Labor Standards Act of 1938 establishes a legal minimum hourly wage for those employed in a large sector of the economy. This mini-

* Reprinted with permission from a symposium, *Anti-poverty Programs,* appearing in *Law and Contemporary Problems* (Vol. 31, No. 1, Winter 1966) published by the Duke University School of Law, Durham, North Carolina. Copyright © 1966, by Duke University.

mum is probably irrelevant for most workers who, even in the absence of the law, would be paid more than the law requires. It is not irrelevant, however, for those in the lowest-skill classes. The law requires that wages paid in some unskilled occupations be higher than the level at which the market would set them. The consequence is that a smaller number of workers is employed in those occupations than would be if there were no minimum wage law, because firms seeking lowest-cost resource combinations are given an incentive to use substitutes for now more expensive unskilled labor. Workers who would have been employed in those occupations but who are kept from them by the law's higher wage standards are either forced into unemployment or enter occupations that are not covered by the law. In these occupations they are worse off than they would have been. . . .

2. The National Labor Relations Act establishes procedures to determine whether workers in a "bargaining unit" desire to be represented by a trade union and, if their decision is affirmative, requires that firms negotiate with the relevant union the terms of unemployment. The act promotes trade unionism. If a union is effective (*i.e.,* if it is not innocuous), the rate of wages in the occupations to which it has reference will be higher than the rate that would have prevailed in the absence of unionism. . . . Such a higher wage rate has the same adverse employment consequences and the same depressant effects upon wages paid in other occupations as do minimum wage laws. Some workers (those who *are* employed at the higher rates) are privileged at the cost of other workers. . . .

3. Farming in the United States is a declining occupation, measured by the relative numbers of persons employed in it. The outmigration from farming is responsive to superior earnings in other sectors, and the relatively low earnings in agriculture can be taken as a proxy for relatively low productivity of employment in agriculture. Output for the economy as a whole would be larger if fewer persons were employed in agriculture and more in other sectors. At least since the middle of the 1930's, public policy has subsidized farmers at the expense of the rest of the community and this has had the effect of diminishing the rate of outmigration from agriculture. Whatever induces people to remain in agriculture will have adverse output consequences and, thus, will tend to enlarge the quantity of poverty.

4. The Social Security Act requires most employed persons to purchase an annuity which is paid to them after they have reached a qualifying age but only if they substantially retire from employment. The annuity is withheld from those older persons who continue to work. The specific form of the rule is that the annuity will not be paid to those whose earnings from employment exceed a specified number of dollars in a year. . . . Some older persons who would be otherwise disposed to continue to work are induced by the law to stop. If they do not stop, they may not have their annuity benefit. The output of the whole economy is, therefore, less by some magnitude; the smaller the output, the larger the quantity of poverty. And the policy precisely induces older people to earn less. The act generates poverty among the aged.

*   *   *   *   *

7. A policy of equal-pay-for-equal-work for men and women is common among the states. Such a policy makes it less attractive for firms to employ women rather than men. It is a policy that fávors men over women by assuring men that women will offer them less competition for employment and that damages women by driving them to unemployment or to second-best employment options. Women who are heads of families are made worse off by it.

8. The incidence of poverty rises with rising numbers of children in the family. Whatever encourages parents to produce more offspring will produce more poverty. While the magnitude of the effect may not be large, the policy of granting exemption from income tax for children when computing tax liability will tend in that direction.

9. The amount of poverty in a community is a function of the quantity of goods and services it produces in some time period and of the distribution of income. Given the distribution, the more that is produced the less poverty there will be. . . . Some welfare payments to the poor and some unemployment benefits, by providing substitute "earnings" for those that would be yielded by work, diminish incentives to work and cause output to be smaller. . . . Unemployment benefits received under some insurance systems are especially vulnerable in this respect since the failure to work is precisely a condition for their payment.

What Do You Think?

1. Would poverty be lessened if these various laws were repealed? Explain your answer. Consider each argument. What points would you offer in rebuttal?

2. Would you agree with the statement, "Given the distribution, the more that is produced the less poverty there will be"?

3. Professor Rottenberg argues that women are hurt by the law requiring that they be given equal pay for equal work. Would most women oppose or support this law? How can this be explained?

6. Faces of the Poor*

Poverty can also be understood in individual terms. The physical and mental characteristics which a person inherits may limit his ability to compete successfully in a modern urban society. Other individuals who are born without any such limitations may be reduced to poverty because of some accident or misfortune that overtakes them. Still others may find themselves poor just because they have grown

* David A. Durfee. Based upon composite cases. See similar sketches in "The Hundred Neediest Cases," *The New York Times,* each December, and Arthur Simon, *Faces of Poverty* (St. Louis, Mo.: Concordia Publishing House, 1966).

too old to work. The sketches which follow illustrate biological limitations and misfortunes.

Francis

Francis appeared to be perfectly normal at birth. His parents were delighted by his arrival for they had wanted a child for some years. The father was a bus maintenance man working in the garage of the local transit company. His income was adequate but there was not much left over after regular living costs had been paid. The mother had encountered a series of illnesses which had both used up all of the family cash reserves and prevented them from having children earlier. When Francis was born, his father was 39 and his mother 36.

As an only child, he was the object of a great amount of attention at home. His parents tried to be with him as much as possible and to anticipate his every desire. When Francis was slow in standing up and in developing the ability to manipulate his toys, neighbors told his parents that it was because they did everything for the boy. In any case, he was not far behind the average child. The parents did worry, however, for they had ambitious plans for the boy. He was certainly to go to college and then into business or perhaps even into a profession. They wanted him to have all of the advantages that they had not had.

At five Francis entered kindergarten and then went on to the first grade. His progress was reported as "normal" for the first three years of schooling, however teachers complained that he was very slow in following directions that were given to the class. In third grade he started dropping behind, especially in reading. His parents became quite upset, and Francis was aware of this. He became more and more disruptive in school. The mother and father talked about withdrawing him from public school and sending to a private one where he would receive special attention, but continued illness by the mother made this financially impossible. The situation at home became more and more tense, and his relations with both teachers and students at school continued to deteriorate.

Tests given at the school revealed two things. The first was that his hearing was somewhat below normal, a condition which had apparently existed since birth and probably explained his slowness in following instructions. The second was that his I.Q. tested out to about 87. It became clear to the parents that their great ambitions for him would never be realized.

Francis failed to pass sixth grade and had to repeat the year. When the class was divided into groups based on ability in the eighth grade, he was placed in the slowest track. When he failed English, social studies, and math in tenth grade and it became obvious that he would lose another year, he gained his parents' reluctant consent to quit school.

After two years of part-time yard work and other odd jobs he moved out of his parents' apartment, which he now found intolerable. For a short period of time he found steady employment at $1.40 an hour with a gas company crew

A college volunteer works with a blind woman at a center in Nashville, Tennessee.

laying down new pipelines. The work was hard and there was no chance for advancement, given his educational background and limited intelligence. Living alone proved to be expensive, and he quit the job hoping to find something better.

Since that time he has had a few temporary jobs, has had three brushes with the law, although not serious, and has become more and more discouraged. His home is now a bug-infested rooming house in a slum area.

Louise

Unlike Francis, Louise was a completely normal child. Her I.Q. was 110 and her hearing and sight were all that they should be. In school she was in the upper third of her class. She was attractive and energetic. Life looked very promising—until she was 13. There was an automobile accident. Her mother was killed, her father was crippled, and she was very seriously hurt. The doctors did all that they could but could not erase the scars on the left side of her face, and they found it necessary to replace her left eye with a glass one.

While the insurance money lasted, a housekeepr took care of the father, and Louise returned to school. It was different now, however. Most people tried to be kind, but she could sense a feeling of revulsion.

When she turned sixteen, Louise left school. This was partly because of the behavior of the students and partly because her father's money had just about given out and she was needed at home to care for him. Since that time she has thought occasionally of taking night secretarial courses but fears that it would be useless because no one would want her in an office anyway.

The money is gone now and they have applied for welfare assistance.

What Do You Think?

1. Are there any other things besides the limited I.Q. and hearing with which Francis was born that might explain his current poverty? Could he have overcome these handicaps? Could you have?
2. Did the school do all that it could to meet Francis' needs? Explain your answer.
3. Would it have made any difference in Louise's case if her parents had been very wealthy before the accident?

ACTIVITIES FOR INVOLVEMENT

1. Make a study of the want ads in your local paper over a period of a week or more. Determine and report to the class on:
   a. How many ads there are for jobs which do not require special skills.
   b. How many of the ads for unskilled labor appear day after day. Is this evidence that there are jobs that no one is willing to take?
   c. How many of the unskilled jobs are seasonal ones and how many appear to be permanent?
2. Select an area of the country other than Appalachia in which there is a great amount of poverty. Do some research into the history of that area and write an explanation of the historical reasons for poverty there.
3. Select one of the areas of "access" discussed in the article "No Access to 'Access'." Using materials on American history as sources, write a description of the methods that have been used to deny this particular access to blacks. Is there more access in this area now than there has been in the past?
4. Do some research into automation. List the arguments that indicate that technological progress will provide more jobs and those that indicate that it will destroy more jobs than it creates. Which set of arguments is more convincing? Why?
5. Write an editorial responding to Professor Rottenberg's article. How would you support one of the laws that he criticizes?
6. Professor Rottenberg says, "Given the distribution, the more that is produced the less poverty there will be." Find out what the current gross national product is. What increase in the gross national product would be needed to raise the income of a family from $2,000 a year to $4,000 a year if distribution remained the same? **73**

6
WHAT ARE
THE EFFECTS
OF POVERTY?

It is easy to see and to understand the economic effects that poverty has on the poor themselves. They must put up with an inadequate diet, with substandard housing, with doing without the goods and services that everyone else seems to enjoy in the affluent society.

Are there other effects, however, that may be less visible but just as serious —effects that hurt not only the poor but all other members of the society and which may even endanger the country? What, for example, is the effect of poverty on respect for law? On family life? On education? On loyalty to country? If poverty weakens these, then it does more than economic harm. The first four readings in this chapter should help you to draw some conclusions about these questions.

Is poverty a major cause of violence, whether in the form of rioting as in the 1960s or in the form of terrorist kidnappings and hijackings as in the 1970s? If so, then it can clearly present a danger to the whole nation. The fifth and sixth readings in this chapter consider this.

Finally, does poverty have any good effects on the society? Are there any values or attitudes that have been preserved among the poor, for example, which are important for America to retain? The last reading in this chapter tells what some might be.

Taken altogether, the selections in this chapter should help you to draw your own conclusions about the effects that poverty has on the poor, on those in the society who are not poor, and on the country itself.

1. "My Husband Got 5 to 15 Years"*

There are several different ways in which crime and poverty may be linked. The following article describes one of them.

My husband is only 21. He was working at Whitaker Manufacturing Company as a machine operator. But he broke his hand before he was eligible

*Excerpted from Kenan Heise, *They Speak for Themselves* (Chicago, Ill.: The Young Christian Workers, 1965). Copyright © 1965 by Kenan Heise. Used by permission.

for the insurance there. He went in on a Monday morning with his hand and tried to work, but they wouldn't let him.

We tried to get by. He tried to work through a day labor office, Ready Man, and even took the cast off himself to do it. We had to let a family take our two-year-old little boy temporarily.

Tom found out that the man was beating our son and we took him right back.

I guess Tom got frantic because of it and because I am expecting next month. Anyway, I can't claim what he did wasn't wrong.

First they caught him in a house he had broken into. Then, while he was out on bail, they caught him on a double armed robbery. He held up two cleaning stores.

It cost us $300 for bail and for the attorney just for the pre-trial hearing. It would have cost us $500 more for the trial, except we got a public defender. He told Tom to plead guilty.

He got 5 to 15 years. It was so much.

I want right now to get an attorney who will review the case. I will go to work right after I have the baby so I can pay him.

It was so much it couldn't be fair.

What Do You Think?

1. Was there anything that Tom could have done to meet the needs of his family other than turn to crime?
2. His wife said, "It [the verdict] was so much it couldn't be fair." Do you agree with her? How do you define "fair" in such a situation?
3. Might the verdict have been different if Tom could have afforded an outstanding lawyer? Explain.

2. The Fourth Summer: The Grady Family*

Why are migrant workers unwelcome and kept out of sight? What effect does the migrant way of life have on the family, on the migrants, attitude toward law, and on education?

That fourth year up the road turned into the scrappingest season the Gradys ever spent. Addie could feel her tongue lash out and she couldn't stop herself. It wasn't only with Henry; her tongue sharpened with the children too.

*From Louisa R. Shotwell, *The Harvesters: The Story of the Migrant People.* Copyright © 1961 by Louisa R. Shotwell. Reprinted by permission of Doubleday & Company, Inc.

It was queer how that awful aching love you could have for a person could show itself only in hateful words.

The heat made things no better. That summer Pennsylvania and New York in July felt hotter than any place Addie remembered in Georgia or Florida. It was the kind of heat that laid a great weight on your arms and legs and took away every bit of tucker you ever had. In every single camp they went to all seven of them slept and dressed and cooked and ate in one room; when it was ten foot by fourteen, it was a big room.

They had running arguments.

They argued over should they open the door and the window and fight the flies or should they shut the door and the window and fight the heat. Whichever way they decided, it didn't make any difference; they found themselves fighting heat and flies and each other all at once.

They argued over should they specialize in beans or should they pick at anything that came along. Henry wanted to specialize; being a specialist, he said, gave a man dignity. Addie said who did he think he was? . . . All right, so if he was [the President] he could specialize in being President of the United States, but if he was Henry Grady he just better crawl along after whatever crop he could find that could use him. Time was Addie could say something like that in a tone that made it three-quarters gentle spoofing and one-quarter serious; now when she said it the words sounded one-quarter serious and three-quarters plain mean. And all the time she was saying them she yearned to take him in her arms and comfort him, but she never did.

They argued should they let the kids work in the fields. Most of the parents had their children work. It sure did add up to more pay tickets when you did, and you couldn't say the extra money wasn't manna in the wilderness. Of course, some places you had to watch out for the inspector. There were special words you called out if you saw him coming, and everybody knew what the words meant; everybody, that is, but the inspector. Matthew thought this was a great joke, and he and Roosevelt set to figuring out a game. The children played it over and over again and taught it to the other kids every time they went to a different camp. The game went like this:

Roosevelt would shout, "Pickin' time," and all the children would drop to their knees on the ground and begin crawling along, making motions with their hands, pantomime-like, at picking beans, and they would singsong:

Pick the ol' beans and *drop* 'em in the basket,
Pick the ol' beans and *drop* 'em in the basket,

and all the while Roosevelt stood turning around and round with his hand shading his eyes, looking and looking at the edge of the sky, and then all of a sudden he'd yell, "Pick 'em clean, Joe," and every child would throw himself flat on the ground and bury his face in the dust. Then from nowhere would come Matthew limping along, dragging his poor clubfoot and managing to swagger and strut, and he and Roosevelt had a little conversation.

Matthew: "Hi, Mr. Row Boss."

Roosevelt: "Hi your own self, Mr. Inspector."

Matthew: "How's the beans, Mr. Row Boss?"

Roosevelt: "Not good, not bad, Mr. Inspector. Just about like they ought to be."

Matthew: "Any kids working here?"

Roosevelt: "Kids? What kids?" (Twisting his head in all directions.) "I don't see no kids. Do you?"

Matthew: "No, no kids. Thank you, Mr. Row Boss, sir, thank you, so long."

And Matthew would limp away; whereupon the little bean pickers would all jump up and race after him and tackle him and down he would go in a heap of tangled arms and legs.

Sometimes the dialogue would get more elaborate. They would discuss the weather in detail, walk up and down examining the bean plants, stepping carefully over the prostrate children, and they would inquire after the health of each other's wives and children.

The first time Addie saw them play it she thought it was cute; times after that a notion nagged at her that it might not be just right for children to be playing at cheating the law. But what was right and wrong anyway? What was the law? Some places there was a law and inspectors and children weren't supposed to work; or sometimes it seemed to be all right if they worked until they were twelve or fourteen and then they had to go to town and get working papers; other places it was all legal no matter how young or old they were. If the law was the law, why didn't it work one place the same as another?

Henry said children ought to work. It wasn't good to leave them back in camp alone, and besides, it was a healthy thing for kids to work, beans or onions or crops like that or picking up potatoes after the machine. They couldn't begin too young, and it was a sure thing they had to learn what it was like because they'd never have a chance to do anything else all their lives long.

This was when Addie really sounded off. So they wouldn't ever have a chance to do anything else, would they? Well, her children weren't going to grow up to be nothing but stooping, crawling bean pickers on the season. They were going to get educated, never you mind how; they were going to train for something good and real, something where you wore a necktie or a uniform and used your head along with or maybe instead of your hands and stood up straight behind a counter or carried a tray or walked a beat or sat down in a chair with four legs in front of a desk and wrote words plain and clear on a typewriting machine. They were going to be somebody and they were going to belong somewhere.

Right there to her astonishment and chagrin Addie found herself crying. Henry said, "Hey, there," and looked so stricken that Addie said, still cross, "Oh, all right, so you're so crazy about having them pick, let them pick, but only just so long as there isn't any school around for them to go to. When we get to a camp where regular school's going on in town and the bus comes by, or where there's one of those summer schools for migrant kids, then they're going to school, understand? No more picking!"

Way back in the spring down in Florida they'd argued over which crew leader to join up with. Henry wanted to go with Digger. Two summers ago they had traveled with him, and he had really rooked them good; couldn't Henry remember that? How he'd promised them 75¢ a hamper for beans, and when the time came he said sure, he was paying 75¢ a hamper, but he had to take out 20¢ for his own share for getting them the job and 5¢ to pay on what they owed him for supplying food all the way up (that food was nothing but soda pop and crackers and sausage and cold baked beans out of a can) and for giving them credit at the camp store before the work began (six days it was, because of the steady rain, before the heat wave brought on the beans in a rush). And he charged them a dollar apiece when they crossed the James River ferry from Little Creek to Kiptopeke when everybody knew it was just 86¢ a person, and when they complained he said if you don't like it you know what you can do. And when they ended up the season with no money at all, he claimed they still owed some (Addie was convinced they didn't but she had no proof) but they were such good people, he said, he'd just forget it. Rubbish!

This year he'd promised them a camp like a motel, with a real "rec" room and television and a cook truck that went right into the fields every noon with hot lunches. "And how much would he take out of our pay for all that?" asked Addie tartly. Henry persisted. Digger had got himself two buses this year to transport his crew; bus riding, said Henry, was sure a whole lot more comfortable than traveling in the back of a truck.

Digger owned an electric razor and he dressed flashy. He was a sweet talker and slick, and when Henry listened to him he forgot all about the crooked treatment of two years back. Henry was just like a child. The very sight of Digger put Addie's back up; as for Digger, he kept a wide berth from Addie. "He knows I see through him," she said to herself.

There were other reasons, too, why Addie didn't want the family to get tied up with Digger. He had a roving eye, and his eye had lit on Lottie. In the four years she'd been on the road with them Lottie had come to be a right pretty eighteen. She fitted nice into the family.

* * * * *

No, they did right to stay away from Digger's outfit and stick with Cap.

The beans were running good, and soon there would be potatoes. The Gradys settled into the camp routine. Up at five, get the family stirring, send Roosevelt out to stand in line at the nearest spigot and fetch a bucket of water, heat up some wash water and last night's coffee, get the grits cooking. (A good thing they'd brought along that little old oilstove and didn't have to crowd into the cook shanty and fight for a spot on a wood-burning cookstove.) Lottie took charge of Princess Anne, bathed and dressed her and fixed her some powdered milk with a little coffee in it. Roosevelt and Sister spread up sandwiches for lunch, and somehow everybody got some breakfast down and turned up ready for the truck at six.

They worked for half a dozen different growers, and sometimes they had to ride forty, fifty, seventy-five miles to get to the fields. Then it was kneel and **79** pick and pick and pick; change to a crouch and pick and pick; go back to kneeling and crawling; get your hamper full, collect your ticket and stuff it deep down good into your pocket, back again to pick, pick, pick. If you stopped to rest, you only felt hotter and stiffer when you started in again.

On the ride coming back the truck would stop at a roadside stand where they had a little store and the people would pour out and cash their bean tickets for cans and cold cuts and cookies. Addie liked to get potatoes and onions and canned tomatoes and pork butts and stew them all together in a kettle; sometimes it was neck bones and rice and black-eyed peas. Canned mackerel with cabbage and corned bread was good too. One night Addie would get dinner and Lottie would do the family wash, and the next night they would trade chores. Evenings there was nothing, just nothing to do but sit in the doorway or on the ground looking for a breath of air that wasn't there, till you got sleepy enough to fall on a straw-stuffed mattress and go out like a light, not caring was the window open or shut.

The heat hung on.

What Do You Think?

1. Will the Grady children ever get to school? Is Addie's dream of their working on jobs where they can wear a tie or a uniform a reasonable one? Explain.

2. In what ways was poverty the cause of the family quarrels?
   Does having the whole family living together in one room make it a more closely knit unit or divide it? What evidence can you find in the story to support your answers?

3. What lessons about laws are the Grady children learning?

3. Let America Be America Again*

There is a contrast between the America that the poor are told about and dream of and the America that is a reality to them.

Let America be America again.
Let it be the dream it used to be.
Let it be the pioneer on the plain
Seeking a home where he himself is free.

(America never was America to me.)

*Reprinted by permission of Harold Ober Associates, Inc. Copyright © 1938 by Langston Hughes. Renewed.

Let America be the dream the dreamers dreamed—
Let it be that great strong land of love
Where never kings connive nor tyrants scheme
That any man be crushed by one above.

(It never was America to me.)

O, Let my land be a land where Liberty
Is crowned with no false patriotic wreath,
But opportunity is real, and life is free,
Equality is in the air we breath.

(There's never been equality for me,
Nor freedom in this "homeland of the free.")

Say who are you that mumbles in the dark?
And who are you that draws your veil across the stars?

I am the poor white, fooled and pushed apart,
I am the Negro bearing slavery's scars.
I am the red man driven from the land,
I am the immigrant clutching the hope I seek—
And finding only the same old stupid plan.
Of dog eat dog, of mighty crush the weak.

I am the young man, full of strength and hope,
Tangled in that ancient endless chain
Of profit, power, gain, of grab the land!
Of grab the gold! Of grab the ways of satisfying need!
Of work the men! Of take the pay!
Of owning everything for one's own greed!

I am the farmer, bondsman to the soil.
I am the worker sold to the machine.
I am the Negro, servant to you all.
I am the people, worried, hungry, mean—
Hungry yet today despite the dream.
Beaten yet today—O Pioneers!
I am the man who never got ahead,
The poorest worker bartered through the years.

Yet I'm the one who dreamt our basic dream
In that Old World while still a serf of kings,
Who dreamt a dream so strong, so brave, so true,
That even yet its mighty daring sings
In every brick and stone, in every furrow turned

That's made America the land it has become.
O, I'm the man who sailed those early seas
In search of what I meant to be my home—
For I'm the one who left dark Ireland's shore,
And Poland's plain, and England's grassy lea,
And torn from Black Africa's strand I came
To build a "homeland of the free."

The free?

A dream—
Still beckoning to me!

The land that never has been yet—
And yet must be—
The land where every man is free.
The land that's mine—
The poor man's, Indian's, Negro's, ME—
Who made America,
Whose sweat and blood, whose faith and pain,
Whose hand at the foundry, whose plow in the rain,
Must bring back our mighty dream again.

Sure, call me any ugly name you choose—
The steel of freedom does not stain.
From those who live like leeches on the people's lives,
We must take back our land again,
America!

O, yes,
I say it plain,
America never was America to me,
And yet I swear this oath—
America will be!
An ever-living seed,
Its dream
Lies deep in the heart of me.

We, the people, must redeem
Our land, the mines, the plants, the rivers,
The mountains and the endless plain—
All, all the stretch of these green states—
And make America again!

What Do You Think?

1. When the poet used the word "America," was he referring to a place or to an idea? What evidence can you find?

2. The poet says:
   "I am the people, worried, hungry, mean—
   Hungry yet today despite the dream.
   Beaten yet today—O Pioneers!
   I am the man who never got ahead,
   The poorest worker bartered through the years."
   This poem was written during the Depression. Would it be any different if written today?

3. Are there any ways in which the feelings about poverty and lack of opportunity expressed in this poem could hurt the society? Explain.

4. Seven Marks of Poverty*

If poverty only affected the lives, attitudes, and institutions of the poor, that would be serious enough, but it does more. The following article describes seven ways in which poverty puts its mark on the entire society.

Poverty among almost a fifth of our people is both root and offshoot of inadequate schooling, deficient health services, crime and juvenile delinquency, inadequate social security and welfare programs to deal with the problems of broken homes and the penury of so many of the old, indecent housing conditions, civil strife, and high unemployment resulting in the main from slow economic growth.

For one thing, this: Today, with an estimated 16 million children among the families of the poor, parents everywhere are discovering that children from urban or rural slums bring the scars of their poverty when they enter the schools. Without pride—or cause for pride—in their backgrounds, they carry indifference and destructiveness. They bring the limited vocabulary of their unschooled parents. They have trouble understanding the teaching. Through their impact upon other children, all of us pay the bill for long neglect. In addition, youths aged 16 and over are more than three times as likely to

*Excerpted from Leon H. Keyserling, *Progress or Poverty: The U.S. at the Crossroads* (Washington, D.C.: Conference on Economic Progress, 1964).

leave school when the family income is under $5,000 as when it is $7,500 or higher.

For a second thing, this: If anyone proposed a scheme to put out of action one-third of the young men who might be needed to defend the nation, he would probably be tried for treason. Yet, Selective Service reported in 1963 that *half* of the young men taking the pre-induction tests had failed. The causes were physical or intellectual deficiencies, or both. President Kennedy appointed a task force to study the facts. It found that, even if all our young men who became 18 in 1962 had taken the tests, *one-third* would probably have failed. Among the sample group of rejectees studied, eight out of ten were school dropouts, and half of these had left school to help support their families; almost half of those who failed to pass the intelligence test came from families with six or more children. The rate of unemployment was about double the rate for all men in the same age group. And most of the young men who failed lost almost their last chance to get the training and discipline, by customary methods, necessary for many industrial jobs. They thus lost their chance to break out of poverty.

For a third thing, this: Some areas of our growing cities are unsafe for women and children even during the daytime, and unsafe for all at night. Crimes of violence of all types are perpetrated largely by those whose early years have been thwarted by poverty or deprivation. Involuntary idleness turns many toward social aberration. And juvenile delinquency increases as the economically handicapped children drop out of school and fail to find work. . . .

For a fourth thing, this: Poverty and all its burdens are highly concentrated among those who must be helped by social programs, because in the very nature of things most of them cannot help themselves—children in broken homes, young female heads of families who cannot work or earn much if they do, and above all, in the tragedy of their penury, millions of our senior citizens. . . .

For a fifth thing, this: Poverty frequently means living under slum conditions, whether in big cities or on the farms. It means overcrowding and lack of privacy; sharing plumbing facilities with scores of others; unique exposure to disease and mental breakdown, with no money to call the doctor; paying more rent than the family can afford; exploitation by high-pressure salesmen who force upon them cars and home furnishings at usurious[1] interest rates and often repossess them. And these living conditions drive children into the streets. There, in addition to all else, more fortunate neighbors may treat them with scorn, blame them for their wretchedness, and cut down their self-respect.

For a sixth thing, this: . . . Just so long as poverty and unemployment are

84 [1]Too high.

so highly concentrated among Negroes and other minority groups, it is only reasonable to anticipate that a quality of desperation will continue to attach to the Negro's appeal to the conscience of his fellow citizens. Civil rights laws, granted their imperative necessity, do not in themselves create additional jobs nor reduce poverty. And just so long as people of different-colored skins have to compete for the scant jobs which mean food and shelter, we'll go on having racial tensions.

And for a seventh thing, this: Apart from the other separate factors in poverty, but both root and offshoot of them all, is the chronically high rate of unemployment.

What Do You Think?

1. The author talks of the impact which the presence of children of the poor in a class has on other school children and of the scorn with which these poorer children are treated by people who are more fortunate than they. Does this suggest that there should be separate schools just for poor children so that they would not have to mix with others? Are there advantages to this idea? Disadvantages?

2. In recent years the standards for admission into the armed forces have been changed so that young men with poverty backgrounds can be taken in and given a chance to make up their deficiencies while serving. What do you think of this idea?

3. Do the poor really have a "unique exposure to disease and mental breakdown"? Explain your reasoning.

5. Poverty and Rioting*

In the last half of the 1960s there were riots in dozens of American cities. Some people saw racism as the primary cause, others poverty. Some claimed that radicals or subversives were at fault.

There was a riot in Newark, New Jersey, in July 1967. To what extent was poverty, absolute or relative, a cause?

Newark

Founded in 1666, the city, a part of the Greater New York City port complex, rises from the salt marshes of the Passaic River. Although in 1967 Newark's population of 400,000 still ranked it thirtieth among American municipalities, for the past 20 years the white middle class has been deserting the city for the suburbs.

In the late 1950's, the desertions had become a rout. Between 1960 and 1967, the city lost a net total of more than 70,000 white residents. Replacing them in vast areas of dilapidated housing where living conditions, according to a prominent member of the County Bar Association, were so bad that "people would be kinder to their pets," were Negro migrants, Cubans, and Puerto Ricans. In 6 years, the city switched from 65 percent white to 52 percent Negro and 10 percent Puerto Rican and Cuban.

The white population, nevertheless, retained political control of the city. On both the city council and the board of education, seven of nine members were white. In other key boards, the disparity was equal or greater. In the central ward [where the city government planned to clear 150 acres of ghetto and let the state build a new medical and dental college despite the opposition of the Negro residents], the Negro constituents and their white councilman found themselves on opposite sides of almost every crucial issue.

The municipal administration lacked the ability to respond quickly enough to navigate the swift changing currents. Even had it had great astuteness, it would have lacked the financial resources to affect significantly the course of events.

[After describing the way in which the flight of the white middle class from the city had cut down on its ability to collect taxes to meet its needs, the *report* continues.]

Consequently, there was less money to spend on education. Newark's per capita outlay on schools was considerably less than that of surrounding communities. Yet within the city's school system were 78,000 children, 14,000 more than 10 years earlier.

Twenty thousand pupils were on double sessions. The dropout rate was estimated to be as high as 33 percent. Of 13,600 Negroes between the ages of

*Excerpted from the *Report of the National Advisory Commission on Civil Disorders* (Washington, D.C.: U.S. Government Printing Office, 1968).

16 and 19, more than 6,000 were not in school. In 1960 over half of the adult Negro population had less than an eighth grade education.

The typical ghetto cycle of high unemployment, family breakup, and crime was present in all its elements. Approximately 12 percent of Negroes were without jobs. An estimated 40 percent of Negro children lived in broken homes. Although Newark maintained proportionately the largest police force of any major city, its crime rate was among the highest in the Nation. In narcotics violations it ranked fifth nationally. Almost 80 percent of the crimes were committed within 2 miles of the core of the city, where the central ward is located. A majority of the criminals were Negro. Most of the victims, likewise, were Negro. The Mafia was reputed to control much of the organized crime.

Under such conditions a major segment of the Negro population became increasingly militant. Largely excluded from positions of traditional political power, Negroes, tutored by a handful of militant social activists who had moved into the city in the early 1960's, made use of the antipoverty program, in which poor people were guaranteed representation, as a political spring-board. This led to friction between the United Community Corporation, the agency that administered the antipoverty program, and the city administration. . . .

The Profile of the Rioter

The typical rioter in the summer of 1967 was a Negro, unmarried male between the ages of 15 and 24. He was in many ways different from the stereotype. He was not a migrant. He was born in the state and was a lifelong resident of the city in which the riot took place. Economically his position was about the same as his Negro neighbors who did not actively participate in the riot.

Although he had not, usually, graduated from high school, he was some-what better educated than the average inner-city Negro, having at least at-tended high school for a time.

Nevertheless, he was more likely to be working in a menial or low-status job as an unskilled laborer. If he was employed, he was not working full time and his employment was frequently interrupted by periods of unemployment.

He feels strongly that he deserves a better job and that he is barred from achieving it, not because of lack of training, ability, or ambition, but because of discrimination by employers.

He rejects the white bigot's stereotype of the Negro as ignorant and shiftless. He takes, great pride in his race and he believes that in some respects Negroes are superior to whites. He is extremely hostile to whites, but his hostility is more apt to be a product of social and economic class than of race; he is almost equally hostile toward middle-class Negroes.

He is substantially better informed about politics than Negroes who were not involved in the riots. He is more likely to be actively engaged in civil rights efforts, but he is extremely distrustful of the political system and of political leaders. . . .

[In describing the typical counter-rioter (those who urged rioters to "cool-it"), the report states that, "he was considerably better educated and more affluent than either the rioter or the noninvolved."]

National Guardsmen on duty in Newark in the morning after the worst night of rioting in that city in 1967.

What Do You Think?

1. Was poverty a major cause of the Newark riot? Was it *the* major cause? What evidence can you find in the articles on riots to support your answers?
2. Do poor people have a right to disobey a law if they feel that it is unfair to them? Explain.

6. Violence and Poverty in the 1970s

In March 1973, leaders of the American Indian Movement (AIM) occupied the small village of Wounded Knee on the Pine Ridge Indian Reservation, holding hostages and defying the U.S. government. Wounded Knee was selected as a symbol of white injustice and cruelty to the Indian. On December 29, 1890, 350 Indian men, women, and children, all of whom had surrendered and most of whom had been disarmed, had been fired on by troops. Only 51 Indians, all wounded, are known to have survived.

The photograph on the top of the next page shows a government bunker on the very spot that served as the command post of the cavalry in December 1890.

On February 22, 1974, the "People in Need" program began distributing over $2 million worth of free food in California, one consequence of the kidnapping of heiress Patricia Hearst by the Symbionese Liberation Army (SLA). The SLA justified the kidnapping as being necessary to do something about the plight of the poor in America. In order to get her captors to begin to talk about releasing his daughter, Randolph Hearst was required to show good faith by mounting a gigantic food distribution.

Some areas in the state saw scenes such as that in the picture below. In the meantime, Miss Hearst renounced her family and stated that she had joined the SLA to fight for the poor and oppressed.

1. Are people like the leaders of AIM or the SLA sincerely convinced that their actions are necessary and just? What other reasons might they have for what they do?

2. Is such use of violence likely to increase or decrease in future years?

3. Does such use of force mean that any future efforts to end poverty will be looked upon as giving in to threats?

7. Yesterday's People*

Up to this point all of the readings in this chapter have focused on harmful or allegedly harmful effects of poverty. Are there any good effects? Are there, for example, any behavior patterns or values that poor people have that more affluent Americans might profit from? The following selection describes some of the values of the poor in Appalachia.

Never have I seen a mountaineer "lording it over" another because he has a new car or a new job or a new house. This kind of materialism is completely rejected. Mountaineers want to have their status based not on objects but on their individuality within their own group. . . .

There is an offhand attitude toward money, almost as if it did not matter, which is in strong contrast to the middle-class striving for money as a goal in itself. Having a certain amount of money obviously does matter, since life itself depends on it, but I have seldom seen a mountaineer who seemed to care how much he was able to get or to save. Other things are much more important to him.

A similar disregard for time is also part of the mountain man's make-up. He lives by rhythms other than the hour, day or week. The rhythms of the shifts at the mine, of hunting and fishing seasons, of gardening—these provide the paces for his life. The particular hour of the day is of less concern to him than it is to the middle-class person.

His person-orientation makes him much more aware of his person-to-person relationships than of a time schedule which must be kept. He cares far more about keeping a friendly relationship with a neighbor whom he has met on the way to a meeting than about being there on time. This is one very important point that middle-class persons must be aware of as they have dealings with mountain people. In the middle-class world, a man can impersonally do what business needs to be done with a person, then proceed else-

*Excerpted from Jack E. Weller, *Yesterday's People: Life in Contemporary Appalachia* (Lexington, Ky.: University of Kentucky Press, 1965). Copyright © The University of Kentucky Press. Used by permission.

where. In the folk culture, you don't just stop in for a moment to check on a detail or two of business, then move on. Each contact is a person-to-person encounter, and this takes time—hours of it. A trip to the store, going to the neighbors' to borrow a cup of sugar or an ax, meeting a friend on the road— these are not impersonal encounters, in which the business at hand can be done quickly, but are occasions for the kind of personal relationships that form the very core of the mountain man's existence.

A county school official recently discussed his efforts to see three men who were being chosen for a special training program. It took him six hours, because—as he noted—"you can't do business with these people on a time schedule." You must also "set a spell," and in the midst of this person-to-person meeting any business you may have can be done. The impersonal manner of business dealing common to the middle class simply will not do for the mountaineer.

What Do You Think? ───────────────────────────

1. Are these characteristics peculiar to mountaineers, or are they characteristics of poor people in general? Have you encountered people with these characteristics?
2. What effect would it have on the society if these attitudes disappeared from it? If they were adopted by all?
3. Are these attitudes the result of the mountaineers' poverty or a cause of it? Explain.

ACTIVITIES FOR INVOLVEMENT

1. Review all the readings in Chapters 3 and 4 as well as in this chapter, looking for evidence on the relationship between poverty and family life. Decide if poverty has any effect upon the family. Write a paper supporting your conclusion.

2. A judge in Washington, D.C., remarked: "From my own experience, I know that most of the defendants convicted of crimes of violence, in the District of Columbia are indigent.[1] A successful war on poverty would come close to solving the crime problem." Collect all the articles on crime in your local newspaper for one week. Study them and then tell whether they tend to support the judge's idea or contradict it.

3. Which *three* of the following would be most affected by poverty that exists in the society? In what ways?
   a. A middle-class suburban housewife.
   b. A wealthy businessman.
   c. A teacher in a rural school.
   d. A teenage girl living in a luxury apartment in the center of a city.
   e. A policeman assigned to patrol duty in a city.

   Be prepared to defend your choices.

[1]Poor.

4. The America that Langston Hughes talked about in his poem was proclaimed in the Declaration of Independence, the Preamble to the Constitution, the Bill of Rights, and other great American documents. Refer to these documents and list the statements which describe this "America." Which of the ideals have we come closest to achieving? Which have we still to accomplish? Is the existence of poverty contrary to these ideals? Explain.

5. Do research to find the eventual results of the AIM occupation of Wounded Knee and the SLA kidnapping of Patricia Hearst. Did these actions help or hurt the poor?

6. Country and western music has become more and more popular in recent years. Select three such songs. Study the lyrics and decide what values they emphasize. Write a report indicating whether these are values missing in affluent urban life in America.

7
WHAT CAN
WE DO ABOUT
POVERTY?

In its extreme American version, inequality is not only grossly unethical, it is also politically dangerous to a healthy democracy.

Robert Lekachman

If poverty, whether it is absolute or relative, has so many effects upon the poor and upon the entire society and almost all of them are bad, what can and should be done about it? Can poverty be eliminated and inequality lessened?

There are people who argue that if we were really serious about doing something to end poverty we would have succeeded in eliminating it by now. Some even believe that the affluent majority in America wishes to preserve poverty. One says:

In present day America, the middle class is defined largely by the fact that the poor exist. Doctors are middle class, but so are bookkeepers; factory workers vacation with lawyers, drive bigger cars than teachers, live next door to store-owners, and send their children to school with the children of bank tellers. In a middle class so diffuse, with almost no characteristic common to all, middle-class income, education, and housing are what the poor do not have. If the present poor should become middle class, no meaning would remain to that phrase. . . . The middle class knows that the economists are right when they say that poverty can be eliminated if we only will it; they simply do not will it.[1]

In 1965 when Walinsky wrote this there was fairly universal agreement that the American economy could continue to climb almost indefinitely. The question was whether or not the poor would receive a larger share of the increasing plenty. By the middle of the 1970s, on the other hand, shortages of resources, inflation, and competition from other manufacturing nations had led a number of Americans to believe that the period of ever-increasing affluence was over and that America would have to tighten its belt in the future.

[1]Excerpted from Adam Walinsky, "Keeping the Poor in Their Place: Notes on the Importance of Being One Up," in Arthur B. Shostak and William Gomberg (eds.), *New Perspectives on Poverty* (Englewood Cliffs, N.J.: Prentice-Hall, Inc., 1965).

Would such a change improve the position of the poor, either relatively or absolutely, or increase their suffering?

Writing in 1974, Robert Lekachman, Distinguished Professor of Economics at Herbert H. Lehman College in New York City, reviewed two new studies of measures that had been taken through the years to lessen poverty. He reported that the conditions of the poor tended to improve during times of full employment and that the gap between the rich and the poor became wider in times of recession. He also reported that the evidence showed that to be popular with the affluent majority of Americans a program had to appear to offer benefits to everyone, not just the poor. For example, by the 1970s there were few who still challenged the Social Security program since everyone grew old and even fewer who questioned aid to the victims of floods and tornados since there was no telling whom such disasters might strike. Welfare programs, on the other hand, were subject to almost constant criticism.[2]

What can and should be done about poverty?

Programs which have been tried and new ones being proposed can be divided into roughly two categories: welfare and antipoverty. Although the line between these two groups is not always very clear and there are some activities that can be listed in both, there is a fundamental difference. Welfare actions are actions designed to solve specific problems of poor people. Giving enough food to someone who is hungry is a welfare action, as is providing shelter for a homeless family. The problems may be solved but the people are still poor after the action has been taken. Antipoverty activities are ones designed to bring individuals and groups out of poverty and into the mainstream of American affluence.

1. Welfare: Problems and Possibilities*

Private and religious organizations and individuals have been involved in welfare operations in America since early colonial days. Large-scale governmental activity in this field, however, is a twentieth century phenomenon. Here are some things that are being done:

There are today dozens of federal laws and hundreds of state and local ones providing for welfare assistance. The total expenditure for governmental welfare programs passed the six billion dollar mark in 1966 and has been rising rapidly ever since then. The federal government provides more than 50 percent of the funds.

Most of the federal programs provide assistance for people who are unable to take care of themselves for some obvious reason. The largest federal pro-

[2]Robert Lekachman, "What Works, What Doesn't," *The Nation,* May 11, 1974. Typical of the critiques of the welfare system is Clayton Thomas, "The Welfare Dollar Goes 'Round and 'Round," *National Review,* January 18, 1974.
*David A. Durfee.

gram, for example, is Aid to Families with Dependent Children, or ADC. Under this program the federal government gives grants to states, and the states distribute the money among families in which the parents cannot, for one reason or another, meet the needs of the children. If there is an able-bodied male in the household, the family is unlikely to receive aid. This feature has made ADC the target of frequent criticism. For example:

> While the law concerning Aid to Dependent Children was originated as a means of supporting children when the head of the family cannot, the prevalent interpretation among the poor is that a family can only receive adequate assistance if the family head deserts.
>
> An unskilled restaurant employee lives apart from his East Harlem family and dodges their case worker so his family can collect full welfare benefits without deductions for his $65-a-week salary. "We have seven kids," he said. "Welfare don't give enough."
>
> Mrs. Esther Medina, a mother of two from Monterey, Mexico, . . . said her husband had worked steadily until he arrived in New York City.
>
> "He was not working and the men on the corners told him he would have to leave home so his family could get welfare. Welfare should not make men desert their families," she said.[1]

Those who support this interpretation of ADC charge that unless it is enforced men will refuse to work and will, instead, live off the payments made to their children.

Other federal programs involve aid to such groups as the blind, the crippled, and the elderly. These programs are carried out by the Department of Health, Education and Welfare.

People who do not fit into any of these federal categories must depend upon state and local governments for funds. Welfare benefits in the most generous states, primarily those in the northeast, are several times as high as those in the most niggardly ones, like Mississippi. Officials in the higher benefit states have expressed the suspicion that the other states deliberately keep benefits low to encourage the unemployables to move out. This compounds the problems of the states which make larger payments.

Recipient families often receive funds from several different programs. Since the different programs are run according to a variety of rules and one program may be made more or less liberal while others remain the same, recipients are often completely unable to understand why they receive as much (or as little!) as they do and suspect that someone is cheating them. The lives of some welfare recipients in New York City, whose welfare provisions are among the most generous in the nation, were described in the article "Life on Welfare" in Chapter 3. The short selection "Welfare: The Starch Diet" shows a welfare mother in Boston in 1974.

[1]Excerpted from Thomas A. Johnson, "Life on Welfare," *The New York Times,* December 19, 1966. Copyright © 1966 by The New York Times Company. Reprinted by permission.

Some details in the life of a welfare recipient like Mrs. White in 1974 were better than those in the mid-1960s, but others were worse. Inflation was obviously hurting the poor, and the housing situation, which had been bad in 1965, had become desperate following years in which more housing units were abandoned or torn down than were built.[2] On the other hand, the federal government had greatly expanded its food stamp program so that, by 1975, an estimated 15.8 million Americans had their diets supplemented by food obtained with stamps.

What Do You Think?

1. A city can cut down on the number of people who are receiving welfare improperly if it hires enough inspectors, but the inspectors' salaries may cost more than the welfare money saved. Should enough people be hired to keep all ineligible people off the rolls even if it costs more in the long run?

2. Should the federal government take over all welfare aid so that no recipient would have a reason to move from one state to another in an effort to get higher benefits?

3. Do unemployable people have a right to adequate welfare benefits? Who should pay?

2. Want Amid Plenty*

In the 1960s America had a food surplus. A federal food stamp program was adopted as a relatively inexpensive way of helping the poor. Depending on income, they would pay part of the face value for the stamps and then turn them in for full value in food. In the 1970s the number of people using stamps increased rapidly, but so did food prices and criticisms of the program.

The house was a faded gray, squatting in the dust beside a crumbling macadam street.

In one of its two rooms Mrs. Luteller Peters, 84 years old, her eyes fiercely bright in a face deeply seamed like black leather stitched loosely over bone, sat under a sign that said in crude red letters: "We reserve the right to refuse service to anyone."

The sign, a relic from an old restaurant, is a grim reminder of years of indignities met by Mrs. Peters as a black in the South and yet another indignity

[2]Albert A. Walsh, "U.S. Faces Recession In Housing Production," *The New York Times,* February 17, 1974.
*Excerpted from "Hunger in U.S. A Problem of Want Amid Plenty," by Willima Robbins, *The New York Times,* October 29, 1974. Copyright © 1974 The New York Times Company. Reprinted by permission.

that she encounters now. Despite billions spent by the government on food aid, she is living out her days in hunger.

A local volunteer agency, aided by Federal funds, delivers a hot lunch to Mrs. Peters every day. But she says she cannot use food stamps for the rest because she is too feeble to go to the store with the coupons, which she says local merchants insist she must present in person. And to provide morning and evening meals for the whole month, she has only $9 of her own available.

Thus, in one of the most fortunate of nations—one with a wide margin of plenty in a world where more than 400 million people suffer malnutrition and many live on the edge of famine—hunger persists.

And while it is a much smaller problem on the whole in this country than in many others, it is no less harsh for the individuals who endure it.

Hunger in the United States has many faces. It exists, a trip into two randomly chosen areas shows, among all types of the poor—the young and the old, the urban and the rural.

Many Young and Jobless

Many of the hungry are elderly and rural, like Mrs. Peters and like Cornelius Butler, 70, who sits through each long day, weak and underfed, on a rotting porch near Jacksonville, Ark.

But there are also many in the cities who are young, angry, unemployed and confused, like William Parish, 27, who is white and who has only bread and peanut butter to eat in his house in Little Rock, or like a black mother of three in Detroit, who survives on the same fare.

The hunger persists even though great sums of money—$4 billion this year—are spent on food stamps under a Congressional mandate to administrators to give the eligible needy "an opportunity to obtain a nutritionally adequate diet" and to try "to insure the participation of eligible households."

And there is much evidence indicating that the situation is worsening because of inflation. Hunger-related crimes, for example, are reported increasing and food stamp applications are reported up sharply in many areas.

Yet, 10 years after passage of the first food-stamp legislation no one really knows how big the problem is.

Such evidence as exists is based on limited studies—limited in both scope and depth. But that evidence indicates that millions of Americans are hungry at least part of their lives, that many suffer from malnutrition, and that many children in the United States suffer permanent mental and physical damage as a result.

Recent testimony before the Senate Select Committee on Nutrition and Human Needs alleged that 37 million were poor enough to be eligible to receive food stamps, with only 14.1 million now receiving such assistance.

Other estimates have ranged as high as 50 million people in eligible families.

The 37-million estimate given in the Senate testimony, as it turns out, stemmed from a projection by an economist at the Department of Agriculture, who based his work on census data.

That projection is now disowned by officials of the department, who point out that figures on incomes reported by census-takers are undocumented and that many of those represented by low-income census figures would be ineligible for food stamps because of assets held, because they are served by institutions, or for other reasons.

Acknowledging, however, that there might be "a high degree of correlation" between the census figures and the number of eligible people in low-income families, one official said: "The truth is we really don't know how many there might be."

The officials also say that food-stamp figures themselves are misleading, because the rolls change constantly. As many as 20 million people may be served during the year, they estimate.

One of the best and the broadest studies of the effects of hunger and dietary deficiencies resulting from poverty is a "Ten-State Nutrition Survey," produced by the Department of Health, Education and Welfare. Though it is now dated, reaching only through 1970, it was based on clinical examinations, and thus is revealing.

40 Percent Affected

The survey found evidence, for example, of deficiency in Vitamin A in more than 40 percent of children of the low-income black families studied compared with 10 percent or less among children of white families.

It also found that more than 8 percent of the low-income black families studied showed evidence of iron deficiency.

As an assumed result of malnutrition, it found that children from low-income families tended to show retarded development, including smaller head sizes. Other studies have shown that young children suffering from malnutrition are penalized throughout life by retarded brain development.

Thus, specialists say, poverty and the blighting effects of poverty are passed on from one generation to another. . . .

In this country, few deaths are reported as malnutrition or starvation. But numerous "high nutrition risk" cases result in early deaths from a variety of common diseases, experts say. . . .

Critics of the basic program for the hungry, the food stamp plan, say that the problem lies partly in the legislation itself. It provides for a "nutritionally adequate diet," but regulations drawn up by the Department of Agriculture relate such a diet to its "economy food plan."

That plan is a carefully selected and measured list of foods designed to provide the minimum needs of basic nutrients. It is "technically possible," one Washington official said, for a shopper to get an adequate diet with a food stamp allowance based on the plan, but it is practically impossible for the poor and often poorly educated families to make the meticulous calculations required in shopping to fill their needs.

In addition, inflation is racing far ahead of adjustments in the food-stamp allowances. . . .

Failure Charged

It is difficult for poor families to set aside enough money to pay at once for the stamps after paying such basic costs as rents, utilities, medical expenses and other necessities that cannot be bought with food stamps.

But more serious problems of hunger persist, the critics say, because of failure of both the Department of Agriculture and local officials who are responsible for distribution of food stamps.

They say the department has failed to impose on responsible local officials the legislative requirement of an "outreach" system to find eligible hungry but nonparticipating families and try to insure their participation.

At the local level, they say, the problem is also administrative, with too few social workers generally to handle the program.

"It's an administrative morass," said Ronald Pollack, director of the Food Research and Action Center, an organization that has filed many lawsuits seeking improvement of the system. There are too few workers and too few offices, he said, and applicants have to travel long distances, sometimes for several days in succession before managing to get through long lines of people waiting for certification. "The working poor just cannot afford all that time," he added. . . .

Telling of long lines and days of waiting that discouraged applicants for aid, the Rev. William Cunningham, a Roman Catholic priest who is director of a volunteer Detroit agency called Focus: Hope asserted: "the programs seem programmed to fail." . . .

Among those getting assistance was a 70-year-old widow, Mrs. Estella Smith, who explained why she could not take full advantage of the program.

Her rent and utilities absorbed all but $70 of her Social Security and welfare checks, totaling $194 a month, she explained. With medical and other expenses, she had available only $16.50 of the $33 that would be required for a full monthly stamp allowance with a face falue of $46.

With the $23 worth of stamps that she can buy, she explained, she survives toward the end of the month on oatmeal and "pots of greens I cook up."

Wistfully, she added: "I can see plenty of people buy so much groceries it's pitiful. I just stand there and look at it."

But far hungrier was a young mother, living with her three children on the top floor of the building pocked with broken windows. She was out of work since being laid off at a restaurant several weeks earlier. . . .

100   She and her children had been living, like the young man in Arkansas, on homemade bread and peanut butter. Focus: Hope came to her assistance with emergency supplies.

Waiting Room Crowded

The young Little Rock man, Mr. Parish, was encountered in a welfare office, waiting angrily in his third attempt to see a worker and gain certification for food stamps. The waiting room was crowded with about 50 other applicants, many of whom gave similar accounts, some with repeated long and costly trips.

The office serves an entire, sprawling county. . . .

What Do You Think? _____

1. Should the government make it easier and simpler for people to get and use food stamps? What steps could be taken to improve the administration of the program?
2. Inflation in food prices has made the program much more expensive than in its early days. If food prices continue to increase, should the stamp program be expanded or cut down? Why?

_____

3. What Must Be Done*

Here Senator George McGovern (Dem., S.D.) reports on the recommendations in a National Nutrition Policy Study completed by a U.S. Senate panel in June 1974, and tells what he thinks the government should do about hunger.

In order to meet the immediate needs of the malnourished and hungry poor in this country, the panel recommended a number of remedies. Among the most significant are the reduction or elimination of the "charge" for food stamps, the reorganization of administration procedures, and the extension of outreach efforts to inform and serve the poor.

The panel also called for a comprehensive evaluation of the food assistance programs. Such an evaluation should include at least three facets: (1) quantification of nutritional benefits; (2) a study of how well present programs are reaching those in need; and (3) a study of needs based on the responses of the participants themselves. This should include an evaluation of the food itself. Food uneaten, no matter how nutritious, has no impact on nutritional

*Excerpted from "An American Paradox: Hunger in an Affluent Society," by George S. McGovern, *Social Education,* November–December 1974.

status. Many cultural minorities have tastes that do not fit in with foods prescribed under regular federal programs. School lunch programs are perhaps the best example of food that often is discarded because of its unacceptable nature or its preparation.

I personally believe that the establishment of an independent Office of Nutrition in the Federal government is critical to establishing national nutrition policy and priorities. Under President Kennedy, I headed the Food for Peace office, which coordinated our overseas food assistance program. The State Department, the Treasury, the Budget Bureau, and the Department of Agriculture were all involved in the program. Building on the experience of coordinating the overseas programs—which I think worked very well—we might think in terms of an office to give a positive new direction to national efforts to eliminate hunger and malnutrition in our own country.

At the classroom level the first priority should be education about the facts of hunger and poverty in America. But nutrition education is almost equally imperative; for while inadequate nutrition is an inevitable corollary to poverty, even many affluent Americans are poorly nourished because of ignorance about basic nutrition. With these two goals in mind, it is important that the United States develop a comprehensive National Nutrition Policy. Such a policy—to be developed in the proposed National Office of Nutrition— should include adequate assistance for the needy in an efficient and dignified manner and adequate nutrition education for us all.

What Do You Think?

1. What effects might proper nourishment of the poor have on the society?
2. Would a combination of knowledge about nutrition and adequate federal funds to make food available solve the problem of hunger in America? Explain.
3. Is it the government's responsibility to see to it that hunger is ended?

4. Self-Help Programs*

Welfare and food stamp programs are run by the government for the poor. While these were a part of the War on Poverty, an even greater part was providing opportunities for the poor to organize to help themselves.

This selection looks briefly at two such efforts. The first is the Community Action Program set up in Syracuse, New York. The second is the effort by migrant farm workers in California to form a union to get wages high enough to lift themselves out of poverty.

The Crusade for Opportunity

The Office of Economic Opportunity was created during the Johnson Administration to coordinate all of the nation's antipoverty efforts. One of its main undertakings was to encourage poor communities within the various cities to form corporations which would receive federal funds to run the kinds of programs the people themselves wanted. The guidelines set by the OEO called for "maximum feasible participation" by the poor in decision making and required that at least one-third of the members of the board running the corporation be poor people.

The Community Action Program in Syracuse took the name the Crusade for Opportunity. The emphasis was placed on programs for youth such as Head Start which provided pre-school training for children from disadvantaged homes. All seemed to be going well, at least to outside observers. Then, in January 1967, a group of militant representatives of the poor gained control of the corporation and voted enough new "poor" members in to assure themselves of continuing control. They declared that this was "maximum feasible participation."

Protests against actions taken by the Crusade under this new leadership were not long in coming. Many of the older service organizations ended their support. Members of the board of directors publicly opposed the new leadership and were suspended. Financial confusion and race and class hatred increased.

*David A. Durfee.

103

OEO finally ended its financial support to the Crusade in October, 1967. Antipoverty programs in Syracuse were either cut back or eliminated entirely. Control by the poor had led to the downfall of the Crusade for Opportunity.

Why was this the result? Militants argued that when representatives who wanted real instead of token improvements for the poor took control, the establishment decided it had to kill the Crusade to protect itself. It accomplished this by hindering the Crusade from within and by working against it from the outside to get funds and support cut off. Opponents of the militants argued that those misleaders of the poor deliberately destroyed the Crusade to discredit the government and create a more revolutionary atmosphere. Less partial observers argued that it was not a case of evil intentions on either side but rather a problem of poor administration on the part of those who had been denied all previous opportunities to gain experience in that field and of poor communication on the part of middle-class people who had never learned to talk with the poor.[1]

A similar crisis arose in New York City in the fall of 1968 over the actions of the governing board chosen by residents of the poor Ocean Hill-Brownsville District of Brooklyn to run the schools in their area. The objective in creating this small school district within the huge New York City District was to see if community control would lead to better education and thus help disadvantaged children to break out of the slums. The conflict between the governing board and "the establishment," in this case the teachers' union, led to strikes and a dangerous increase in racial tension.

The same interpretations of the trouble were given as were heard in Syracuse: the result of the establishment's attempting to keep the poor down but quiet; the result of militant attempts to promote riot and revolution; and of well-intended mistakes by inexperienced people.

Cesar Chavez[2]

In Coachella, the pickets gather in the dark at three-thirty in the morning. By four o'clock they are on their way to the fields, their long rows of headlights bouncing over the desert roads towards half-a-dozen different vineyards. By dawn they will be strung out along the sandy roadsides, in front of huge square patches of irrigated green in the sagebrush, and they will shout into the fields: *"Huelga!"*

Strike. Harvest and strike have come together in the far south of California. They will go on together through the summer heat, moving north together through the great chessboard grape valleys of California.

Already grapes, and enormous investments, are rotting. Even so, composure is the rule. Occasionally, it gives way to the frantic: a foreman in a pickup truck pinwheels off the road into a knot of pickets idling in the five o'clock heat,

---

[1] A more detailed discussion of this crisis can be found in Lawrence Davis, "Syracuse: What Happens When the Poor Take Over," *The Reporter,* March 21, 1968.
[2] Excerpted from Lincoln Richardson, "Cesar Chavez," *Presbyterian Life,* October 1, 1968. Used by permission.

he scatters several who scramble to safety, and knocks two more painfully aside, then accelerates in the loose sand toward the field: Pickets swarm over the truck, pounding on the windshield, pulling open the doors, throwing sand into the cockpit, bringing it to a stop.

Sudden silence. The fierce foreman, quickly transformed, peers around from behind the wheel, blinking like a man who has lost his glasses; there is a trickle of blood across the bridge of his nose. The creator of silence is a short, erect man, who has just pulled the fiery captain of the pickets off the running board, and now looks easily around a circle of uneasy faces. The anger in the eyes of Cesar Chavez is well-contained in the steady gaze that has looked carefully at conflict and indignity, and is now confident, hopeful, and, always, calculating.

Addressing the ranking grower in the group, who has just driven in from San Francisco headquarters in a sports car, Chavez delivers a short purposeful speech. "This has got to stop. It's happening here. It's happening up north. The San Joaquin Valley is about to blow. We've got to have peace this summer. This has got to stop." In the face of a vigorous round of seconding speeches from the pickets, the grower also keeps his cool: "The foreman was wrong. *I said* he was wrong. What do you want me to do?"

Later, in the calm, the grower, who has shipping interests as well as land up and down the state, mentions that he has heard from an official in the longshoremens' union. The longshoremen have been supporting the pickers' strike; Cesar and the grower retire across the road for a talk. Cesar considers him a good guy with only one serious flaw: he won't sign a contract. "He says he would, but that he can't sign without the others. A lot of them say that."

Cesar climbs back into his car, beside the Reverend James Drake of the California Migrant Ministry, his administrative assistant and closest associate. They will make one more quick tour of the area. They have been cruising rapidly about since four o'clock; at almost six, work is underway. Striking a grape valley is a complex and difficult art, with no successful models. It is like striking a factory thirty miles across with thousands of entrances. Every row is an entrance. The chances of facing workers as they enter the fields are dim; pickets rely on loudspeakers, persuasive rhetoric and a show of numbers to persuade workers to come back out—"Join us, brothers. Leave the fields. Stand up for your rights."

Standing by the road in the early light, the pickets are mostly young, boys and girls who are already veterans at stoop labor. They have slept a short night on the floor, eaten donated food, and now seem exhilarated to be standing beside a field, and holding a red and black flag, ready to begin shouting into the field. Some are older, grayheaded men, who have also slept on the floor, and to whom austerity has already given dignity. Now, in austerity for a purpose, they have gained pride. Theirs is not the half-enchanted garrulity of the young, laced with laughter, but they too will shout: *"Huelga!"* Strike.

It is impossible to know exactly where the pickets should be, but it is Cesar's business, as director of the United Farm Workers' Organizing Committee, to know as much as possible, and he has learned to read the vineyard country well.

Few workers will leave the fields while the pickets are there. Many, however, do not return the next day. When the workers first come into the area —UFWOC openly suspects that many are recruited in Mexico and smuggled across the border—few of them have heard of the strike, or have even imagined a strike of farm workers. Striking has always seemed to be the exclusive privilege of industrial workers: when the Wagner Act in 1935 established the legal basis for workers to organize and bargain collectively, it excluded farm workers. Since then, most growers and workers alike have accepted that exclusion as natural. But now, Cesar Chavez is attempting to gain rights won by everyone else thirty years ago. He appears the more radical to his adversaries because of the very anachronism of his struggle. He is seen, not as a conservative who is thirty years late and trying to catch up, but rather as a radical, daring to challenge a tradition so very venerable. . . .

Next morning, departure for Coachella is delayed by half-a-dozen pieces of business. There has been a personnel problem at the cooperative which, because the automobile is basic to the farm workers' economy, began as a gas station and parts shop. The co-op is run by the Reverend Fred Dresser, a successful grocer, who, after a late seminary education, joined the staff of the California Migrant Ministry. From the co-op, Cesar goes to the large new headquarters the union is building at the edge of town. The union had set up a large cross at the edge of the property; someone has set fire to it during the night. Then, after a second stop at the present office to pick up documents, they are off for Coachella.

The documents are contracts, and Drake reads the terms aloud as they drive south. Cesar does not negotiate contracts. "I can fight with them during a strike," he says, "but once they are beat, I haven't got the heart to negotiate."

Outcomes

By 1975 the Office of Economic Opportunity had been disbanded. A few of the programs it had started had been transferred to the Department of Health, Education and Welfare, but funds for those that were run by the poor, such as the Community Action Program, had been ended.

Also by 1975 Cesar Chavez had discovered that he need not have felt badly about "beating" the growers. In the early 1970s the growers signed new labor contracts with the Teamsters Union rather than with Chavez's group. Convinced that these new contracts would hurt the migrants, Chavez called for a return to the boycott on lettuce and grapes. He was concerned that conditions under the Teamster contract might be as bad as in the old days.

What Do You Think?

1. **Who is in the best position to know what actions are needed to improve the conditions of the poor: government officials, professors, successful businessmen, or poor people? Why?**

2. **What are the main arguments for and against middle class Americans supporting actions like the Chavez strike and boycott?**

5. Proposals for Ending Poverty*

Neither welfare nor self-help have succeeded in eliminating poverty. What, if anything, should be done in the future? The various proposals seem to fall into five categories.

1. No major new programs should be adopted at this time. In such a time of inflation, danger of recession, and worldwide competition the nation must act to keep the economy as healthy as possible. To do this, all efforts should be focused on helping those who are most efficient in the economy, not those who are least efficient. Increase the rate of profit that can be made from investment and production by providing tax breaks and other incentives. If businessmen know that they can make more money by producing more and building new plants, they will do those things. If they build efficient new plants this will help the United States to compete for the world's markets. Increased production will mean more goods available for sale and this will help cut down on inflation. Finally, there will be more jobs available for the poor and they will be able to earn their way out of poverty.

2. Foolish governmental programs which actually encourage poverty should be eliminated or changed. The reading "Misplaced Emphasis in Wars on Poverty" in Chapter 5 described a number of the programs which are criticized as causes of poverty by people who believe that the way to fight poverty is to eliminate the restrictions that presently limit businessmen's freedom of action. The most criticized program of all is welfare, which is seen as hurting the poor and the economy by providing an alternative to work for lazy people.

3. The government should take strong and positive action to end scarcity in America. A leading proponent of this position is Leon H. Keyserling of the Conference on Economic Progress. Professor Keyserling argues that the way to end poverty and other economic woes in America is to achieve a full-employment economy which produces all of the goods that the society needs. There would be jobs for all who could work and enough goods to take care of those who could not, the elderly and the crippled. He argues that freeing businessmen will not accomplish this because they operate on the basis of scarcity rather than of plenty. There is a tendency for them to limit rather than expand production so that prices will remain high and to limit employment so that wages will remain low. He sees this scarcity behavior as responsible for the country's difficulties. If this is the natural behavior of businessmen, then

*David A. Durfee.

eliminating existing government controls would tend to make the situation worse than better.

The professor's proposed solution is the establishment of a "National Purposes Budget."[1] This would determine how many jobs, how much production, etc., are needed for a full-employment economy. The government would then make up any difference between the number of jobs needed and the number provided in private industry.

4. Radical changes must be made. There are those who go far beyond Keyserling in blaming the rich for the condition of the poor. They see the economic power of America concentrated in the hands of a relatively few bankers and manufacturers who use the power to make themselves even wealthier. Some of these critics feel that the only way to end this is through socialism. The government should take ownership of the means of production away from these few greedy people and use the factories, farms, and mines for the benefit of all the people. Other critics, frequently called populists, argue that the way to end the evils is by limiting the amount of wealth and power any group or individual can have. All income in excess of a set limit would be taxed away, and all giant economic combines would be broken up into competing units. Competition would then force prices down. At the same time, there would be increased regulations to protect the health and safety of the consumer and the worker.

5. A single method of income redistribution should be adopted. All of the complicated and sometimes contradictory welfare and aid programs should be replaced by some simple system. The most commonly proposed system is the Negative Income Tax (NIT). This would provide a cash grant to every American. For example, in his 1972 campaign for the presidency, Senator George McGovern proposed a grant of $1,000 per person. The grant program would be accompanied by a tax system. As described by Robert Lekachman in the article mentioned above:

> The defining NIT features are two: a basic cash grant and a tax on earnings. A grant of $1,500 per person would confer an income of $6,000 on a family of four. If the tax on earnings were 50 percent, the tax authorities would recover the $6,000 when family earnings from the job or jobs of its members reached $12,000, but the family would still be subsidized to the extent that they would return the $6,000 and pay no tax on the earned $12,000. Taxes on family incomes, grant plus earnings, above $18,000, would sharply rise.

Every individual would be guaranteed a certain minimum income to use as he wished and the cost would be recovered through higher taxes on larger incomes. The result would be redistribution of income from rich to poor.

[1] Leon H. Keyserling, *The Scarcity School of Economics* (Washington, D.C.: Conference on Economic Progress, 1973).

1. What are the advantages and disadvantages of each of the types of proposals? What kinds of people would be most likely to support each?
2. There is direct disagreement about how businessmen would behave if unrestricted. Which position do you think is correct? Why?
3. Which of the proposals would you support? Why?

6. Rationing and the Poor*

There have been few new proposals for dealing with poverty in the 1970s. This one, by Peter Caws, was proposed in reaction to the energy crisis.

The current crisis draws our attention to something that has been true, although not obvious, for a long time: although this country is rich in natural resources, it is wasting them, and the resources of other parts of the world as well, by its enormous appetite for energy. If America is to be self-supporting in this respect, and also to avoid pollution and the despoiling of nature, not to mention saving some of the resources for future generations, it has to learn to conserve. This means a change in patterns of energy use and hence in personal habits. The problem is how to encourage this change without oppressive legislation.

Inside the country the distribution of energy is skewed, naturally enough, toward the wealthy; a strict accounting would show that most of the energy is spent, directly or indirectly, by the minority that owns most of the money. One of the things that has held up the equalizing of wealth in America, and that has made welfare seem somehow un-American, is a natural and partly justified feeling on the part of the rich and influential that Robin Hood tactics are unfair. The money they use belongs to them and to nobody else, however deserving. And in fact the principles of a democracy say nothing about the distribution of money. They might, however, say something about the distribution of energy. For it is a philosophical truth that a man is not necessarily free, just because nobody is oppressing him; he is free only if he has the resources of energy and information he needs in order to do what he wants to do. So nobody is entirely free—but it is up to the government, in a democratic state, to equalize what freedom there is.

The information is taken care of (in principle) by educational policy; the energy needs a policy of its own. Let us assume that everybody has a right to

* *The New Republic,* December 15, 1973. Reprinted by Permission of *The New Republic,* copyright © 1973 Harrison-Blaine of New Jersey, Inc.

his fair share of the energy resources (not of the money) available to his generation. These resources are, of course, useless unless they are dug up or otherwise processed into a usable form; this has to be done by somebody, by industry for example, and the work of processing deserves to be rewarded. That explains why, even if one has the right to the energy, one still has to pay for it. But if an individual cannot afford to pay for it, still it does not follow that anyone else is entitled to use his share without consulting him. How can his interests be protected?

Suppose legislation were to establish the right of each to his share of energy, and to mandate the issue of vouchers, multiples of a suitable unit, rather as ration cards were issued during World War II. How would such a system work? First of all if an individual wished to buy anything—gasoline, airline tickets, electric power—that represented the expenditure of a significant amount of energy, he would have to spend energy vouchers as well as money. So many units would be attached to each kind of expenditure, according to a scale devised by experts. Nobody would tell anybody what to do, everybody would be free to choose—but not free, in the first instance, to choose to consume more than his share. Some activities—local public transportation, the manufacture and processing of staple foods and other necessities—would be exempt from this accounting, and energy would be freely available up to a modest per-capita level, varying by region, and season, for domestic cooking, heating and lighting.

Now suppose, to take an oversimplified case, two individuals, Smith and Jones. Each has enough energy vouchers to fly to Australia *or* to drive a Lincoln Continental *or* to run a central home air-conditioning system. But Smith is poor; he has the vouchers but not the money; he can't afford to do *any* of these things; in fact he can't afford to do anything much at all, and his energy needs are minimal, falling below the level where the voucher system takes over. Jones, on the other hand, is rich; he wants to do *all* these things, and can afford to, in fact he can afford to do anything he likes; he has the money but not the vouchers.

The obvious answer is for Jones to offer to pay Smith for his vouchers. But Jones lives in Florida and Smith in North Philadelphia; besides, Smith is a less astute businessman than Jones, and if somebody does not protect him he will get a poor deal. An intelligent government would have forseen this, and by setting up an Energy Voucher Exchange (EVE) would have made a fair arrangement possible. EVE would issue the vouchers, but it would also sell them and redeem them; in fact, anticipating the social realities of the situation, it would allow individuals to exercise their energy drawing rights in cash or vouchers according to choice. Some industries, engaged in the production of nonessential goods, would be big customers for vouchers, and so would some wealthy individuals. Even so, when the total supply of vouchers ran out, they would have to stop using energy altogether. And the total would of course have been computed so as to keep the country within its resources. Between this and the cost of extra vouchers, the incentive to live at a lower level of energy consumption would be considerable.

All rationing schemes generate black markets. But here it is not a commodity that is rationed—although bootleg gasoline and heating oil would have to be watched for—but a right. Since every voucher would be personal, or at least accounted for against the name of some person, the scheme would have to ensure the compensation of that person for someone else's use of the voucher, and minimize the possibility of the enrichment of some other person at his expense. So limits would have to be placed also on the purchase of vouchers for unspecified use, and their resale would have to be forbidden.

Finally, the cash equivalent of vouchers would be officially set at a level that any individual who chose to exercise his drawing rights in cash would find himself in command of an acceptable minimum income. If this were done, welfare could at the same time be abolished, and with it the psychologically damaging effects of living on handouts, since drawing on EVE would be a right, part of what it means to live in a democratic state. This would save local governments a lot of money, and also—since vouchers would be redeemable anywhere in the country—remove the incentive to crowd into the cities where the welfare programs are. In fact, because cities are more expensive, it might reverse a demographic trend. The place of the welfare clients in the inner city might in turn be taken by refugees from the suburbs who wished not to spend all their vouchers on commuting. But suburbanites would have other strategies: the drive to the small car is already on, and there would be increasing pressure for voucher-free public transportation. (The exemption of local mass transit systems would of course require a careful definition of "local"; there seems no reason to exempt public inter-city transportation. But in the latter case the voucher cost would be least for trains, more for buses and planes.)

EVE would not be particularly difficult to administer. It would be a large-scale operation but, once the preliminary calculations had been done (setting energy levels for various activities and working out cash equivalents), a relatively simple one. And it might work.

What Do You Think?

1. Do you agree with Mr. Caws that every American has a right to a fair share of the nation's energy?
2. The plan seems quite simple. Can you find any flaws in it? Explain.

ACTIVITIES FOR INVOLVEMENT

1. Have members of the class visit as many governmental and private agencies working in the welfare and antipoverty fields as possible. Find out what programs seem to be working and what programs do not seem to be working and why. Report to the class and use the data as the basis for a discussion of the scope, effectiveness and problems of current programs.

2. If it is not possible to conduct the visits outlined in Activity 1, have groups in the class do research into each of the programs to uncover the information needed for the discussion.

3. Have members of the class form proposals for actions to deal with the poverty situation. Conduct a mock Congressional session in which they are proposed as bills, debated, and voted on.

4. Write an essay answering the question, "Is poverty a personal problem or a national disgrace?"

Donate to food banks, Charities

BIBLIOGRAPHY
For Further Study

BOOKS

BRECHER, CHARLES • *Impact of Federal Antipoverty Policies* • New York, N.Y.: Praeger Publishers, Inc., 1973.

COLES, ROBERT, and AL CLAYTON • *Still Hungry in America* • New York, N.Y.: W. W. Norton and Company, Inc., 1969.

EVERETT, ROBINSON O. (ed.) • *Anti-Poverty Programs* • Dobbs Ferry, N.Y.: Oceana Publications, 1966.

FERMAN, LOUIS A., JOYCE L. KORNBLUH, and ALAN HABER (eds.) • *Poverty in America: A Book of Readings* • Ann Arbor, Mich.: University of Michigan Press, 1965.

GALBRAITH, JOHN KENNETH • *The Affluent Society* • Boston, Mass.: Houghton Mifflin Company, 1958.

GANS, HERBERT J. • *The Urban Villagers: Group and Class in the Life of Italian Americans* • New York, N.Y.: Free Press of Glencoe, Inc., 1962.

GLAZER, NATHAN, and DANIEL PATRICK MOYNIHAN. • *Beyond the Melting Pot* • Cambridge, Mass.: Massachusetts Institute of Technology Press, 1963.

GOTTLIEB, DAVID, and ANNE L. HEINSOHN. • *America's Other Youth: Growing Up Poor* • Englewood Cliffs, N.J.: Prentice-Hall, Inc. 1971.

HAZLITT, HENRY • *The Conquest of Poverty* • New Rochelle, N.Y.: Arlington House, Inc., 1973.

HOFFMAN, PAUL G. • *World Without Want* • Westport, Conn.: Greenwood Press, Inc., 1973.

LEWIS, OSCAR • *La Vida: A Puerto Rican Family in the Culture of Poverty* • New York, N.Y.: Random House, 1966.

MAY, EDGAR • *The Wasted Americans: Cost of Our Welfare Dilemma* • New York, N.Y.: Harper & Row, 1964.

MOYNIHAN, DANIEL P. (ed.) • *On Understanding Poverty: Perspectives from the Social Sciences* • New York, N.Y.: Basic Books, Inc., 1969.

MYRDAL, GUNNAR • *Challenge to Affluence* • New York, N.Y.: Random House, 1963.

RIIS, JACOB A. • *How the Other Half Lives: Studies Among the Tenements of New York* • New York, N.Y.: Charles Scribner's Sons, 1918.

SHOTWELL, LOUISA R. • *The Harvesters: The Story of the Migrant People* • Garden City, N.Y.: Doubleday & Company, Inc., 1961.

SIMON, ARTHUR • *Faces of Poverty* • St. Louis, Mo.: Concordia Publishing House, 1966.

STONE, ROBERT • *Family Life Styles Below the Poverty Line* • Lexington, Mass.: Lexington Books.

WELLER, JACK E. • *Yesterday's People—Life in Contemporary Appalachia* • Louisville, Ky.: University of Kentucky Press, 1965.

WILKINSON, RICHARD G. • *Poverty and Progress: An Ecological Perspective on Economic Development* • New York, N.Y.: Praeger Publishers, Inc. 1973.
WILL, ROBERT E., and HAROLD G. VATTER (eds.) • *Poverty in Affluence: The Social, Political and Economic Dimensions of Poverty in the United States* • New York, N.Y.: Harcourt, Brace Jovanovich, Inc., 1970.
WOYTINSKY, EMMA S. • *Profile of the U.S. Economy: A Survey of Growth and Change* • New York, N.Y.: Praeger Publishers, Inc., 1967.

REPORTS

COLEMAN, JAMES S, *et al.* • *Equality of Educational Opportunity* • Washington, D.C.: U.S. Government Printing Office, 1966.
FORD, THOMAS R. (ed.) • *The Southern Appalachian Region: A Survey* • Lexington, Ky.: University of Kentucky Press, 1962.
Hungry Children • Special Report of the Southern Regional Council, Atlanta, Ga., 1967.
The People Left Behind, A Report by the President's National Advisory Commission on Rural Poverty • Washington, D.C.: U.S. Government Printing Office, 1967.
Report of the National Advisory Commission on Civil Disorders • Washington, D.C.: U.S. Government Printing Office, 1968.

PAPERBACK BOOKS

BALDWIN, JAMES • *The Fire Next Time* • New York, N.Y.: Dell Publishing Company, 1962.
BENNETT, ROBERT, and THOMAS NEWMAN • *Poverty and Welfare* • Boston, Mass.: Houghton Mifflin Company, 1974.
BLISS, BETSY • *Poverty* • Morristown, N.J.: Silver Burdett Company, 1970.
BROWN, CLAUDE • *Manchild in the Promised Land* • New York, N.Y.: New American Library, 1965.
BROWN, DEE • *Bury My Heart at Wounded Knee* • New York, N.Y.: Bantam Books, 1970.
CAUDILL, HARRY • *Night Comes to the Cumberlands* • Boston, Mass.: Little, Brown & Co., 1963.
CONANT, JAMES B. • *Slums and Suburbs* • New York, N.Y.: McGraw-Hill Book Company, 1961.
CONOT, ROBERT • *Rivers of Blood, Years of Darkness* • New York, N.Y.: Bantam Books, 1967.
FISHMAN, LEO (ed.) • *Poverty Amid Affluence* • New Haven, Conn.: Yale University Press, 1966.
GAVIN, JAMES M., with ARTHUR T. HADLEY • *Crisis Now* • New York, N.Y.: Random House, 1968.
HARRINGTON, MICHAEL • *The Other America: Poverty in the United States* • Baltimore, Md.: Penguin Books, 1963.
HUNTER, DAVID R. • *The Slums, Challenge and Response, 2nd ed.* • New York, N.Y.: The Free Press of Glencoe, 1968.
JACOBS, PAUL, *Et al.* • *Dialogue on Poverty* • New York, N.Y.: Bobbs-Merrill Company, Inc., 1967.
116   KERVIN, PETER • *Poverty and Wealth* • Valley Forge, Pa.: Judson Press, 1971.

KEYSERLING, LEON H. • *Progress or Poverty: The U.S. at the Crossroads* • Washington, D.C.: Conference on Economic Progress, 1964.

_____ • *The Scarcity School of Economics: And the Shortages It Has Wrought* • Washington, D.C.: Conference on Economic Progress, 1973.

LARNER, JEREMY, and IRVING HOWE (eds.) • *Poverty: Views from the Left* • New York, N.Y.: William Morrow and Company, 1971.

LENS, SIDNEY • *Poverty—Yesterday and Today* • New York, N.Y.: Thomas Y. Crowell Company, 1973.

MARGOLIN, REUBEN J. • *The War on Poverty* • West Haven, Conn.: Pendulum Press, 1969.

MEISSNER, HANNA H. • *Poverty in the Affluent Society* • New York, N.Y.: Harper & Row, 1973.

POTTER, DAVID M. • *People of Plenty: Economic Abundance and the American Character* • Chicago, Ill.: University of Chicago Press, 1954.

RYAN, WILLIAM • *Blaming the Victim* • New York, N.Y.: Random House, 1972.

SHOSTAK, ARTHUR B., and WILLIAM GOMBERG (eds.) • *New Perspectives on Poverty* • Englewood Cliffs, N.J.: Prentice-Hall, Inc., 1965.

THOMAS, PIRI • *Down These Mean Streets* • New York, N.Y.: New American Library, 1967.

ARTICLES

BAGDIKIAN, BEN H. • "Black Immigrants" • *The Saturday Evening Post,* July 15, 1967.

BENNETT, LERONE, JR. • "Money, Merchants, Markets: The Quest for Economic Security" • *Ebony,* February 1974.

"Hearst Nightmare" • *Time,* April 29, 1974.

"Invisible Poor of the Garden State" • *Commonweal,* September 8, 1967.

"Is U.S. Really Filled with Poverty?—A Reply" • *New Republic,* October 7, 1967.

JACOBS, PAUL • "How It is, Getting on Welfare" • *Harper's Magazine,* October 1967.

LEKACHMAN, ROBERT • "What Works, What Doesn't" • *The Nation,* May 11, 1974.

LEWIS, ANTHONY • "Affluence and Survival II" • *The New York Times,* April 21, 1974.

MAHOOD, WAYNE • "The Plight of the Migrant" • *Social Education,* December 1973.

"Mississippi: Starving By the Rule Book" • *The Nation,* April 3, 1967.

"The New Poverty" • *Series for Economic Education,* Federal Reserve Bank of Philadelphia.

OPHULS, WILLIAM • "The Scarcity Society" • *Harper's Magazine,* April 1974.

ROWAN, H. • "The Minority Nobody Knows" (Mexican-Americans) • *Atlantic Monthly,* Vol. 219, June 1967.

SHERRILL, R. • "It Isn't True That Nobody Starves in America" • *The New York Times Magazine,* June 4, 1967.

THOMAS, CLAYTON • "The Welfare Dollar Goes 'Round and 'Round" • *The National Review,* January 18, 1974.

WILKINS, ROGER • "The War on Poverty: Ten Years Later" • *The New York Times,* June 4, 1974.

FILMS AND TAPES

The American Indian Today (2 color filmstrips with record; *The New York Times*)
• Shows both the cultural heritage the Indian is preserving and the problems he faces today.

The American Poor: A Self-Portrait (2 color filmstrips with cassettes, Guidance Associates) • Pictures and interviews with people living in poverty in rural and urban areas.

At Home, 2001 (30 min; color; Modern Talking Picture Service Inc.) • A part of the *21st Century* series. Shows the direction in which the affluent mainstream of America is moving and provides a good contrast when shown with materials on the poor.

The Battle of Newburgh (54 min; B/W; McGraw-Hill; 2 reels) • An award-winning NBC 1963 "White Paper" presentation examining the struggle over the efforts by City Manager Joseph Mitchell to cut welfare costs in the New York town. Interviews with people on welfare.

Cities and the Poor (120 min. in two parts of 60 min. each; B/W; NET-Indiana University) • Part I examines the conditions, problems, and frustrations of the poor in Chicago and Los Angeles. Part II examines unrest and explores current antipoverty programs and their weaknesses.

Decision at Delano (16mm film, National Education Media, Inc.) • Award-winning film about the strike against the California grape growers led by César Chavez. Includes an interview with Chavez.

Edge of Abundance (60 min; B/W; NET-Indiana University • An examination of the automated and technologically advanced American economy and the impact that such advances have on employment, education, and values.

Environment and the Economy (Color filmstrip with record, *The New York Times*) • Examines the present problem of producing enough to meet the needs of all people without destroying the environment through pollution or exhaustion of resources.

Harvest of Shame (54 min; B/W; McGraw-Hill) • A "CBS Reports" investigation of the conditions under which migrant farm laborers live and the attitudes of more affluent people toward them. Extremely effective.

How Would You Like to Be Old? (2 color filmstrips with cassettes, Guidance Associates) • Considers the way in which the society tends to "discard" its old as well as the special problem that poverty presents to them.

The Migrant Worker (2 color filmstrips with cassettes) • Similar to *Harvest of Shame* in content.

Must the World Go Hungry (Color filmstrip with cassette, Current Affairs Films) • Contrasts absolute poverty in other parts of the world with America's general abundance and explores possible courses of action.

My Own Yard To Plan In (7 min; B/W; Contemporary Films, Inc., New York and San Francisco) • An art film showing children of varying ethnic groups displaying imagination and joy as they play in a slum environment. Challenges the idea that the poor are "they," a group born different and inferior.

Nothing But a Man (92 min; B/W; Brandon Films, Inc., New York, Chicago, and San Francisco) • A feature movie about the struggle of a sensitive, working class Negro in the South to achieve and maintain a sense of his own identity and manhood. Engrossing and effective.